D1474577

FAMOUS AIRCRAFT OF THE
NATIONAL AIR AND SPACE MUSEUM

VOLUME 1
EXCALIBUR III:
The Story of a P-51 Mustang

VOLUME 2
THE AERONCA C-2:
The Story of the Flying Bathtub
(in press)

FUTURE VOLUMES PLANNED:
MESSERSCHMITT 262
LOCKHEED XP-80
ALBATROS DVa

This P-51C skims the tops of Texas clouds, showing off its clean fighter lines. Its birthplace can be seen through breaks in the clouds adjacent to the airfield that is now Naval Air Station Hensley, near Dallas.

Excalibur III
The Story of a P-51 Mustang

by Robert C. Mikesh

PUBLISHED FOR THE
National Air and Space Museum
BY THE
Smithsonian Institution Press
WASHINGTON, D.C.
1978

LIBRARY OF CONGRESS CATALOGING IN PUBLICATION DATA

Mikesh, Robert C.
  Excalibur III.

  (Famous aircraft of the National Air and Space Museum ; 1)
  1. Excalibur III (Airplane)   I. National Air and
Space Museum.   II. Title.   III. Series.
TL686.N6M54   629.13'09   78-606028
ISBN 0-87474-635-3

Designed by Gerard A. Valerio

Printed in the United States of America

Unless otherwise noted, photographs are from National Air and Space Museum
files or belong to the author. All drawings are by the author.

Contents

Foreword

Although many books have been published on the P-51 Mustang over the years, this is far more than just another Mustang book. *Excalibur III* (North American P-51C 44-10947) nearly missed its chance for glory by not being assigned to a combat squadron. Instead of ending up in the boneyard, however, as did so many World War II fighters, it not only went on to amass great racing victories and records but also to develop new navigational techniques for air transportation routes across the top of the world.

Robert C. Mikesh records in exciting detail the history of *Excalibur III* from its brief stint in the Army Air Forces, its racing years in the Paul Mantz stable, its pioneering flights with Capt. Charles Blair at the controls, to its restoration by craftsmen of the National Air and Space Museum to its present pristine condition.

I hope that this book, which contains a number of photographs and marking details of vital importance to model builders, will be of great interest to airplane buffs and aviation historians as well as to casual readers.

Excalibur III: The Story of a P-51 Mustang is the first volume in a new series — Famous Aircraft of the National Air and Space Museum. Each volume will cover the history and some details of the restoration of selected airplanes in this museum's collection.

MICHAEL COLLINS
Director, National Air and Space Museum

Acknowledgments

The author extends his appreciation to those who assisted with the documentation of this historic airplane. First and foremost is Charles F. Blair, who gave his personal accounts about *Excalibur III* for the time he owned it. Don Dwiggins, Dustin W. Carter, Birch Matthews, Don Berliner, Frank Strand, Don Downie, and Clarence L. "Kelly" Johnson were very helpful in providing background information about this airplane when it was a Bendix Race aircraft. Their reviews and comments on the final manuscript, along with those of Frank G. Compton and William T. Barker, added extensively to a more complete and accurate accounting of this fascinating airplane. Hope Pantell did the editing and untangled my words for you, the reader. My thanks to her and also to my wife, Ramona, for her patience and help while this story was in the making.

Excalibur III

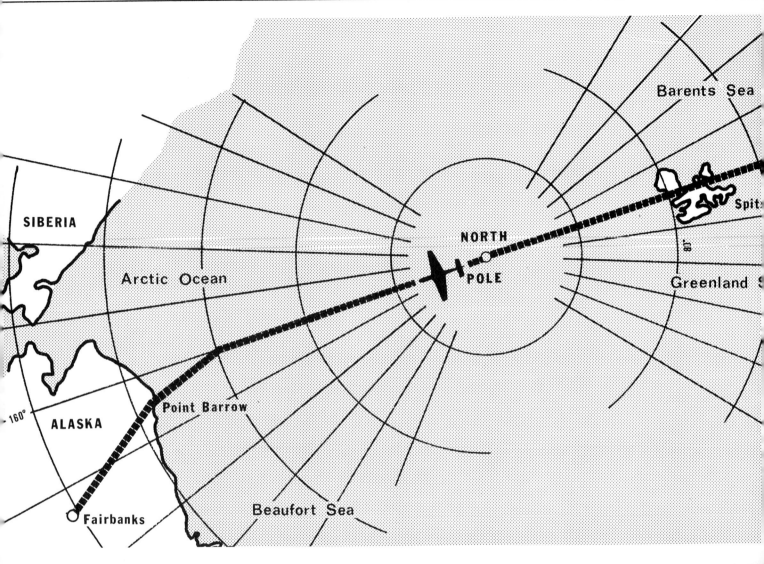

The North Pole was a forbidding place; men had lost their lives trying to reach it. In time, its crossing would be no more difficult than flying any other air route of the world. Creating this link between the past and the future was a P-51C named Excalibur III, flown by Capt. Charles F. Blair. In 1951 they made the first nonstop flight from Norway to Fairbanks—on opposite sides of the world—across the North Pole.

2

A Record of Triumphs

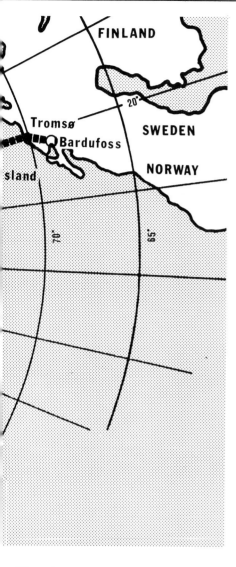

There is every reason for Excalibur III *to have a proud look. This photo, taken in November 1977, marked the end of its restoration, which prepared it once again for exhibit in the National Air and Space Museum (NASM). Its long history includes two first-place finishes in the coveted Bendix Race, the breaking of the transcontinental and transatlantic speed records, and an extraordinary flight from Europe to North America via the North Pole.*

"According to my reckoning, Excalibur III was crossing the top of the world. Now every direction was south. It was like sitting on top of a giant maypole, faced with a pick of countless streamers, one of which leads to Point Barrow, my destination. Others lead to Siberia, to Greenland, or back to Norway, but the choice had long since been made. It meant holding the sun steady off to the left of the airplane's nose, exactly where it had been during the last few minutes before reaching the Pole. This selects and guides me on the correct southbound course of my journey."[1]

These thoughts came to the mind of Capt. Charles F. Blair, Jr., during the historic moment when he made the first solo crossing of the North Pole in May 1951. This flight was not a stunt—it was a well-planned demonstration of his theory of navigation by the sun in polar regions, where the magnetic compass becomes useless. So practical was his new navigational theory that to prove his point Blair made this flight alone in a single-engine airplane—a far cry from the four-engine transoceanic transports he normally flew. His accomplishments in air navigation won for him the Harmon International Trophy in 1952.

The event brought the spotlight of history into focus not only on the man but on the airplane as well. The plane was a North American P-51C-10NT Mustang, named *Excalibur III* by Charlie Blair. Together they set several records that still stand, climaxed by this very significant polar crossing. Immediately after World War II, in the hands of an earlier owner, Paul Mantz, this Mustang achieved a string of victories in the Bendix Transcontinental Air Races. These accomplishments have earned for it a place in the aircraft collection of the National Air and Space Museum in Washington, D.C.

Excalibur III began its service life as a fighter aircraft in the U.S. Army Air Forces on July 25, 1944. Its only identity was its Air Force serial number 44-10947 when it emerged from the North American Aircraft Company plant at Dallas, Texas, the site of the present Vought Corporation facility. In a way, this Mustang, which was a flat-canopied model, started with a disadvantage, for it had already been made obsolete by the bubble-canopied P-51Ds with their better visibility and roomier cockpits. These later models were coming off the production lines at the Inglewood, California, plant of North American, and had reached the combat zone in Europe four months before. Conversion to these newer models was slower at the Dallas plant because of the large number of P-51Cs already in production under contract AC 40063, which called for 2,500 Dallas-built Mustangs of four different types. It took some time, then, to complete the early models already started. The flat-canopied Mustangs would be used, however, for there was little or no difference in performance between them and the later P-51D models.[2]

---

1. Quoted passages relating to *Excalibur III* have been taken from the book *Red Ball in the Sky* by Charles F. Blair (Random House, 1969), with permission of the author.

2. The P-51B(C) was approximately 4 mph faster than the P-51D (both clean configuration) at high blower critical altitude. Tests were run with B-1650-3 engines in both aircraft at 61″ Hg and 3,000 PRM. The B(C) fuselage/canopy configuration had lower drag. The D's advantage was its better visibility.

RIGHT:

When Excalibur III *began its life as a military fighter, it would have looked like this P-51C sister ship, except for its serial number. Many of these fighters were turned out in olive drab camouflage, but late production models left the factory in natural metal, as was the case with our subject aircraft.*

In all, 1,750 P-51Cs were produced, many on the same production lines as the newer bubble-canopied P-51D model. Both models of the Mustang were noted for their smooth, sturdy lines.

Chocks have just been pulled at Eglin Field, Florida, as the pilot gives the thumbs-out signal to the ground crewmen. The Packard-built Merlin V-1650 engine turns an 11'-2" Hamilton Standard propeller, delivering 1,695 hp at takeoff. With the landing gear retracted, the Mustang's frontal area was very small. These qualities made the aircraft an excellent postwar racing plane. (U.S. Air Force)

Combat in the skies over Europe was not in store for the Mustang in this story. Instead, it departed the factory at Dallas on July 29, making an overnight stay at Jackson, Mississippi, and on the next day was flown to Pinellas Army Air Field, Florida, near St. Petersburg, which was to be its new home. This was a Combat Crew Training Station (Fighter) of the III Fighter Command, 3rd Air Force. The mission for this P-51, assigned to the 341st Army Air Forces Base Unit at Pinellas, was not a glamorous one, but the aircraft served the useful function of training fighter pilots for overseas replacements.

The Mustang's next move was on February 8, 1945, when it was reassigned to Venice Army Air Field, south of Sarasota, Florida, for more of the same abuse by pilots of limited experience being readied for combat. The new unit was the 337th Army Air Forces Base Unit, also within the same Fighter Command.

When the war ended, so did military service for '947, after a little more than a year of active duty. On August 26 the Mustang was turned over to the Cincinnati Division of the Air Transport Command to be ferried to a gathering point for surplus airplanes. This movement did not take place, however, until October 5, when the airplane was flown to the Reconstruction Finance Corporation (RFC) facility at Searcy Field, Stillwater, Oklahoma, where it joined acres of other surplus military aircraft. Its days before entering the fiery furnaces of the melting pot seemed numbered, for it was now stricken from the military inventory.

Although the end seemed near, a new lease on life was about to begin for this Mustang. In the hands of the RFC, which was responsible for surplus military property, it would be disposed of in the best way possible. Because of the vast quantities of war-weary airplanes, any one of them could be purchased for a fraction of their original price. Some would fly again, but for most their greatest value was their price as scrap. (P-51 Mustangs were listed at $64,569 when new.)

5

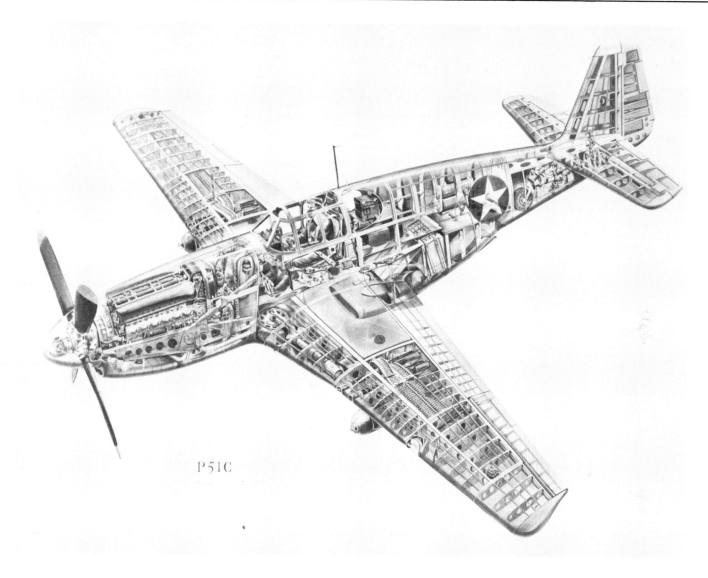

P51C

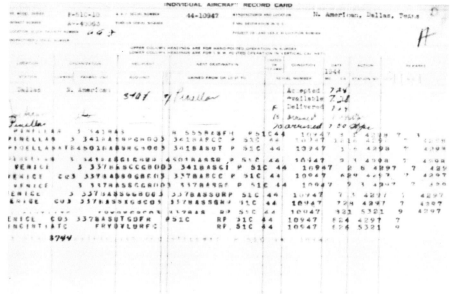

Cutaway drawing of the North American P-51C Mustang in military configuration. (Rockwell International)

LEFT:

This is the military aircraft record card for P-51C, 44-10947, which later became N1202 and is now in the National Air and Space Museum. A record of every Air Force aircraft was kept in this manner, and most are on microfilm by AF serial number at NASM, the Air Force Museum, and the Air Force Historical Research Center at Maxwell Air Force Base, Alabama. They contain such individual data as delivery date, station assignments, modifications, and date stricken from military service.

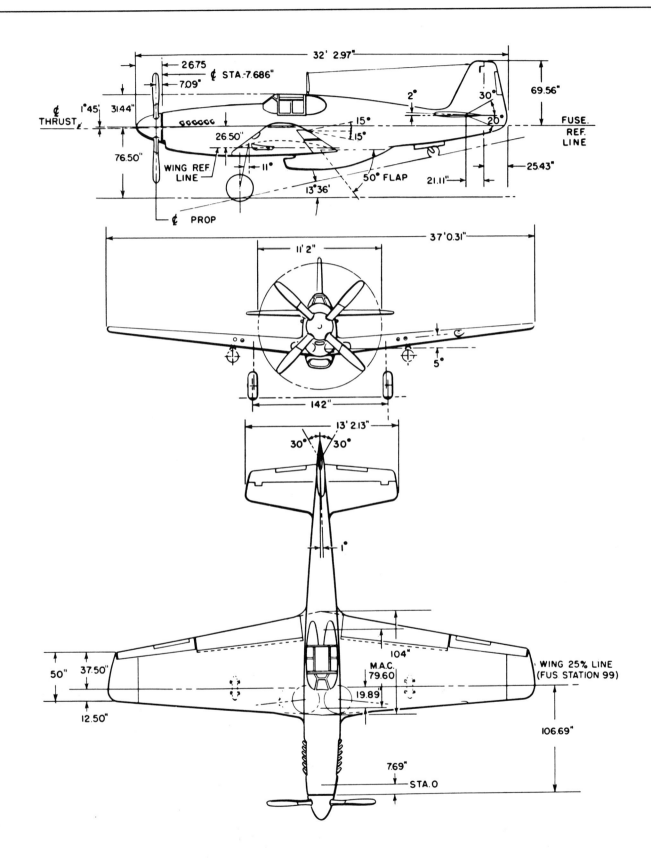

Paul Mantz and His "Air Force"

One of many purchasers of these airplanes was A. Paul Mantz, famous in the aviation world as a flying daredevil for the movies and a pre-World War II race pilot. On one bill of sale Mantz took ownership of 475 airplanes of many descriptions, adding these to his stable of other aircraft. One aviation magazine acclaimed him as the owner of the "world's seventh largest air force."

Such a move by Mantz surprised no one, for in spite of his Errol Flynn good looks and Douglas Fairbanks charm, he was a shrewd businessman. His flying skills, considerable as they were, served only as a basis for business for this man who realized that he had a virtual lock on a very salable commodity—aircraft for the movies. When he viewed his newly acquired armada, he did not see just wings and tails, he saw thirty years of future war films, all of them using his "air force." Those that were surplus to his flying needs were turned into a huge scrapping operation for a sizable profit. The gasoline that was drained from their tanks alone, reputedly was sold for almost as much as the entire cost of the planes he bought.

Two of the best P-51Cs were among the airplanes he kept: one—the subject of this story—44-10947, and the other, 42-103831. These twins were inseparable and followed parallel paths while owned by Mantz. What these fighters had failed to achieve in combat victories over the enemy, they achieved in racing victories never before or since equaled.

Mantz was already a veteran of the prewar Bendix Transcontinental Races, and with the races starting again in 1946 after a seven-year lapse, he was out to win the big money. The Bendix was a long-distance speed dash generally starting in California and terminating in Cleveland, one of the major events of the Labor Day weekend National Air Races. In prewar

OPPOSITE:

Three-view dimensional drawing of production P-51B and P-51C. (Rockwell International)

Initial showing of the former military P-51C occurred during the first year of Paul Mantz's ownership. With registration number NX1202 and race number 46, its bright red finish highly polished, the airplane took first place in the 1946 Bendix Transcontinental Air Race. This gave Mantz his first victory after three prewar attempts. (Dustin W. Carter)

This Lockheed Orion was Paul Mantz's prewar entry for the 1938 Bendix Race. Bright red with white trim and scalloped white rudder was a standard scheme for Paul Mantz Air Service aircraft. This scheme carried over to Mantz's postwar Mustang racer, NX1202. Noticeable side-view difference was the inverting of the fuselage arrow point on the Mustangs. (Dustin W. Carter)

Sister ship to NX1202 was this P-51C NX1204, also owned by Paul Mantz. It was flown by Tommy Mayson, and came in third in the 1946 Bendix Race. Had Mantz's primary aircraft failed before the race, this would have been his fall-back plane. (Rockwell International)

events, each race craft was custom-built and depended on the creative genius of its designer to obtain the greatest speed possible. Now, the wartime technology embodied in surplus military airplanes exceeded that in the one-of-a-kind, hand-made racers, and the challenge was to improve upon these former war machines.

The Lockheed P-38/F-6 Lightning was the most popular type entered in the 1946 Bendix Air Race, accounting for sixteen of the twenty-two entries. The Lightning had been designed as a long-range fighter escort and seemed a natural for the long-distance dash. Mantz and two other pilots preferred Mustangs. Equipped with external drop tanks, all these airplanes were capable of making the 2,048 miles from Van Nuys, California, to Cleveland nonstop, while still maintaining the high-power setting needed to win for the entire flight. All these entries would be close contenders, and Mantz knew that an added ingredient was needed to give him the edge in speed.

He asked his long-time friend Kelly Johnson, the famed Lockheed engineer, for his ideas on solving the problem. Almost matter-of-factly, Kelly suggested plugging up the wings and filling them with gasoline. Lockheed had used this concept on Constellations and the earlier Lodestars, as did North American on prewar BC-1 Harvard Is and SNJ-1s and 2s. No doubt Mantz recalled Frank Fuller's "wet-wing" Seversky of the prewar races. The wet-wing concept would eliminate the need for external fuel tanks, with their attendant drag, that all the other racing fighter planes needed to cover the prescribed distance nonstop. Race pilots would be allowed to jettison the empty tanks, but time would be lost in finding a clear area, for should the tanks inflict damage, the fliers would lose their pilot licenses.

Sold on the wet-wing idea, Mantz proceeded to modify his two P-51Cs by pulling out all unnecessary items within the wing and coating the interior with fuel-tank sealant. This work was accomplished in what seemed like wartime secrecy in a restricted area of Mantz's hangar. The end result of the wet-wing arrangement gave an additional 406 gallons to the Mustang's normal 269-gallon internal capacity, and eliminated the need for the two 150- or 220-gallon external drop tanks.

When Mantz and Thomas J. Mayson, one of the charter pilots flying his second ship, appeared at Van Nuys for the start of the race, other pilots asked them where they would land along the route for fuel. None seemed to believe the truth when told that both Mustangs had wet wings, and could fly the course nonstop without external tanks.

Mantz groomed '947 as his ship for the Bendix Race. It was freshly painted a brilliant red and polished to a high gloss. Its military serial was now forgotten and it carried the white registration numbers of NX1202. The race number 46 was speared by a stripe along its side. In small letters was the name *Paul Mantz,* on both sides of the cockpit, along with the required word *Experimental,* for aircraft in the racing category.

The second Mustang now carried registration number NX1204 and race number 60. Its highly polished fuselage remained natural metal, but its wing had been given the same care as its sister ship. Irregularities in the airplanes' close tolerance laminar-flow wing contours were carefully filled and smoothed, then coated with a mirrorlike finish of bright red.

When the starter's flag went down, NX1202, with Mantz at the controls, was off with a throaty roar, intent on making the fastest time to Cleveland. Pilots who had preceded Mantz at the starting line had had their troubles— and Mantz was no exception. As the airplane's wheels retracted, they snapped against the wheel-well doors, which had closed prematurely out of

An early morning crowd watches the start of the 1946 Bendix Race at Van Nuys, California. NX1202 is not visible in this picture, but its sister ship number 60 is at left. P-38s were favored in that first postwar race, but P-51s took top honors. (Don Downie)

sequence with the system, preventing recycling. The extra drag made it unlikely that the airplane would even finish the race. Climbing to 25,000 feet, Mantz tried to make the best time possible under the circumstances. In one last desperate attempt to solve the drag problem, he depleted the hydraulic pressure and put the Mustang into a tight loop in hopes of forcing the wheels down and releasing the closed doors. At this high altitude for aerobatics, the P-51, with its heavy load of gas, snap-rolled with unexpected force, but the gyrations extended the wheels, and the retraction was then completed.[3] The dash to Cleveland at full military power all the way was made at the most favorable wind altitudes, between 22,000 and 33,000 feet, on an unwavering steady line through summer showers and clear blue sky. Mantz's long, gradual descent at military power was made at a constant 505 mph on the red line until he crossed the finish line. He was the winner with a new speed record for the Bendix, averaging 435.5 mph, covering the

3. This was more dangerous than it sounds. At a roll rate of two radians per second, centrifugal force would bulge the outer wing panels if they are filled with fuel. Hydraulic ram effect could de-skin the wing.

NX1202 leaves the runway at Van Nuys, California, for the dash to Cleveland. Wheels are nearly retracted, but the wheel-well doors closed first, preventing full retraction and nearly costing Mantz the race. (Don Downie)

Flying was a business for Paul Mantz, and he devised a new way for this Bendix-winning Mustang NX1202 to make money. He contracted with Paramount Pictures, which was producing a new movie, "Blaze of Noon," to carry that name on his airplane; thus the corporation could cash in on the publicity at the conclusion of the flight. Mantz set a new coast-to-coast speed record from Burbank, California, to New York of 6 hours and 7:05 minutes. (Don Dwiggins)

A victorious wave is given by Paul Mantz as he greets newsmen at LaGuardia Airport after his transcontinental speed dash. Following the 1947 Bendix Race, NX1202, probably again painted with "Blaze of Noon," established a new east-west speed record of 7 hours and 5 seconds.

Already fueled for the 1947 Bendix Race, NX1202 waits for the early morning start from Van Nuys Metropolitan Airport. Fuel was chilled so more could be packed into the wing for the long, fuel-guzzling run to Cleveland. The blankets kept the fuel from heating and expanding too rapidly on the ground. Changes to the aircraft from the previous year were limited to new and differently shaped propeller blades and a Bendix MN-60A loop antenna below the air scoop. (Rockwell International)

distance in 4 hours, 42 minutes, and 14 seconds. Ten minutes' running time behind him, in second place, was the only woman entry, Jacqueline Cochran, in another P-51C. Tommy Mayson in Mantz's other Mustang, NX1204, finished in third place, just 19 minutes behind the winning ship. The Mantz winnings were $10,000 for first place; $3,000 for third place.

The speed capability of NX1202 had become a moneymaker for Mantz, and he planned new ways to capitalize on it. Although setting speed records offered no monetary gain, Mantz, as a shrewd businessman, recognized the profit that could be gained from the publicity that went with such feats. Knowing that he could beat the transcontinental speed record with his Bendix racer, Mantz contracted with Paramount Pictures Corporation to carry the name of their new motion picture, "Blaze of Noon," on the side of his airplane for advertising purposes.[4] For the first time in the news media, NX1202 was referred to by a name, but it was a purely commercial name. On February 28, 1947, with the strong westerly winter wind pushing the Mustang along, Mantz did set a new west-east record for a propeller-driven, single-engine plane from Burbank, California, to LaGuardia Field, New York: 6 hours, 7 minutes, and 5 seconds. Paramount paid a generous fee to Mantz for carrying the name of the film, and the event achieved the intended publicity.

The challenge was expected to be strong for the coming 1947 Bendix Race that September. Mantz again planned to be the winner with the same Mustang. So sure was he of victory that he matched Houston oil millionaire Glenn H. McCarthy's $10,000, that his Mustang would beat McCarthy's P-38 in the Bendix. The rumors of this bet, whispered among race enthusiasts, added even greater excitement to the coming contest.

When the day arrived, McCarthy's P-38, *Flying Shamrock*, named after his elegant Houston hotel, ran into trouble at the moment of takeoff. The drop tank from the left wing fell free and burst into flames that spread down

4. This was a story of barnstorming in the 1920s and the early days of the Air Mail. Pitcairn Mailwings and Travelaire 4000s were flown for the film by Mantz and his crew of stunt pilots.

In preparation for the 1947 race, extensive work was done on NX1204 to ready it for the grueling grind. Metal seams of the wet wing are being resealed prior to being repainted. At right rear in this Mantz Air Service hangar can be seen the nose that appears to belong to NX1202. (Don Dwiggins)

Paul Mantz's two Mustangs get last-minute checks before the start of the 1947 Bendix Race. Mantz flew number 46, at center, while Tommy Mayson flew number 60, right background. A-26 number 91 (left) is given an engine run-up by a mechanic. Its pilot, Dianna Cyrus, landed in Michigan and did not complete the race. (Don Downie)

As first-place winner of the 1947 Bendix Air Race, Mantz strikes a classic pose for the cameras. This was his second straight win, both victories in NX1202. In three prewar bids for the Bendix Trophy, Mantz finished third in two races. He became legendary not only for his air racing, but as a movie stunt flier as well. His tragic death came in a crash on July 8, 1965, during filming of "The Flight of the Phoenix."

the runway. Undaunted, pilot James Ruble continued on with enough fuel remaining to safely finish the race.

Over Arizona, more serious problems arose for *Flying Shamrock*. With the plane's engines pushing the maximum continuous operating power limit, one of the turbo-superchargers disintegrated, causing an uncontrollable fire, and Ruble was forced to bail out. With this challenger out of the competition, all Mantz had to do was finish the race to win the $10,000 bet from McCarthy.

Winning the Bendix was the real objective for Mantz, and the red Mustang number 46 was the spectators' favorite. And win Mantz did—cutting 16 minutes off the record he set the previous year. He crossed the finish line a mere minute and 18 seconds ahead of the second-place aircraft, a wet-wing P-51, piloted by Joe C. DeBona. Mantz's other Mustang, NX1204, flown by Tommy Mayson again, as the year before, did not fare as well, finishing in sixth place, one hour after its winning sister ship.

The next day found Mantz and his red Mustang, now often referred to as "Blaze of Noon," poised at LaGuardia Airport to dash to the West Coast in an attempt to establish a new east-west transcontinental speed record for this class of airplane. It has not been confirmed if "Blaze of Noon" was again painted on the side of the Mustang, but most likely it was, since Paramount again sponsored the news-making flight. The motion picture industry had long used a water-soluble paint for quick or easily changed paint schemes, and it may have been used for this flight. Pointing the Mustang westward into the low-velocity summer head winds on September 3, 1947, Mantz again captured a record with NX1202, by crossing the continent and reaching Burbank in 7 hours and 5 seconds.

The racing business was expensive, and the $20,000 Mantz had won in the 1947 Bendix was barely enough to keep his two Mustangs in racing condition. Since it *was* a business, Mantz entered into a sponsorship agreement

Mantz is off for the 1947 Bendix Race from California. The landing gear retracted properly in this race, as evidenced by the wheel-well doors having opened prior to gear retraction. (Don Downie)

Following its victory in the 1947 Bendix Race, NX1202 is towed away from the winners' circle at Cleveland. (B. J. Matthews Collection)

17

Sister ship to NX1202 was '04, and both Mustangs appeared at the 1947 Bendix as a race team, the same as the year before. The only change from the previous year for '04 was yellow paint on its fuselage and the added loop antenna housing under the airscoop. Tommy Mayson again flew this ship for Mantz, finishing in sixth place. (Dustin W. Carter)

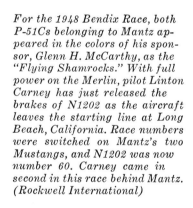

For the 1948 Bendix Race, both P-51Cs belonging to Mantz appeared in the colors of his sponsor, Glenn H. McCarthy, as the "Flying Shamrocks." With full power on the Merlin, pilot Linton Carney has just released the brakes of N1202 as the aircraft leaves the starting line at Long Beach, California. Race numbers were switched on Mantz's two Mustangs, and N1202 was now number 60. Carney came in second in this race behind Mantz. (Rockwell International)

OPPOSITE:
Gathering speed on the takeoff roll, N1202 is off for Cleveland in the 1948 Bendix Race with McCarthy's pilot, Linton Carney, at the controls. He averaged 446.1 mph along the 2,048-mile route; maximum continuous power was maintained over the 4-hour, 34-minute period. Such continuous high-power operation spoke well for the Packard-built Rolls Royce Merlin V-1650 engines. (Dustin W. Carter)

with race enthusiast McCarthy for an advertisement program for his Shamrock Hotel. In return for $75,000 from McCarthy, Mantz would enter his two Mustangs and a third owned by Ed Lunken with the Shamrock colors, promising to win first, second, and third places for McCarthy. Mantz was out to win the Bendix Trophy for the third straight time. McCarthy saw his determination, and accepted the offer. NX1202 then became part of the stable of Flying Shamrocks.

The starting point for the 1948 race to Cleveland was changed to Long Beach, California. This year the covey of Paul Mantz racers sported new color schemes. Instead of the former bright red, all three were in pearl gray. The propeller spinners and tips of the wings and tail were red, and other marking details, including the distinctive shamrock adorning the tail of each Mustang, were green. Since Mantz elected to fly NX1204 in this event, the race numbers of his two P-51Cs were switched so that Mantz could retain his favored 46. N1202, to be flown by McCarthy's pilot, Linton Carney, was now marked with race number 60. This switch in numbers became a continual cause for confusion between the two sister ships in the years that followed.

Race competition was keen, for others were out to beat Mantz for the trouncing he had given them in the previous two years. As promised, however, NX1204 was first across the finish line, averaging 447.9 mph and giving Paul Mantz the distinction of being the first and only winner of three consecutive Bendix races. Our subject airplane, NX1202, flown by Carney, took second place at 446.1 mph, and it seemed that the Shamrock airplanes would come in first, second, and third, for Ed Lunken was closing in on Cleveland very fast. Jackie Cochran wedged in just ahead of Lunken, however, taking third spot in her P-51C, number 13. Mantz failed to bring his Shamrock Mustangs in as planned, but his triumphs were never exceeded in the Bendix, and McCarthy's hotel received the publicity he had bargained for.

For the 1949 Bendix Race, the two P-51s owned by Mantz were in readi-

Colors on Mantz's P-51s in the 1948 race—light gray with medium green markings and dark green outlines—were a drastic change from the red of previous years. Only the propeller spinners and the tips of the wings and tails remained red. Glenn McCarthy sponsored Mantz and his three Mustangs, intending to win the first three money-making awards. The shamrock was to advertise McCarthy's Shamrock Hotel in Houston. N1202 is at rest at the Cleveland airport after the race. (B. J. Matthews Collection)

The sister ship of N1202 was NX1204, now wearing race number 46 instead of the 60 of previous years. The other Mustang of this trio of "Flying Shamrocks" was number 33, a P-51D owned by Ed Lunken, carrying the name "Texan." (Dustin W. Carter)

OPPOSITE:
Paul Mantz has every reason to be proud and have a wide smile in this 1948 picture at the National Air Races. He was the only person to win the Bendix Trophy three consecutive times. The trophy would be awarded only one more time, for the 1949 competition was the last for this race. The Bendix Trophy, now owned by Clifford Henderson, is on exhibit at the National Air and Space Museum. (Robert E. Burke)

OPPOSITE:
The starting line for the 1949 Bendix Race was quite different from previous years. The race-horse start was made from Rosamond Dry Lake in the Mojave Desert in Southern California. There were only six entries that year. Mustangs belonging to Mantz are in the foreground with NX1202 carrying number 60. (Don Dwiggins)

Cleveland Airport was the finish line for the Bendix races, a major part of the National Air Races, in postwar years. While spectators watched other events from these bleachers, they also kept their eyes peeled to the west for the Bendix entries to cross the finish line. The national anthem is being played in this 1949 picture as the Stars and Stripes are raised to start the National Air Races on that Labor Day weekend.

OPPOSITE, LEFT:
Flying for a fourth time in the Bendix races, in 1949, N1202 is once again in the standard Mantz bright red paint scheme, but with an all red rudder. The race number 60 remained the same as the previous year. Herman Salmon flew the ship, finishing third. (Dustin W. Carter)

OPPOSITE, RIGHT:
At rest on the Mojave Desert, N1202 poses for the camera before the 1949 Bendix Race. Once again, the Mantz racers carried the red paint scheme of the Paul Mantz Air Service, covering the gray paint of the previous year. A significant change is that the entire rudder is painted red. (B. J. Matthews Collection)

ness, painted in their original red with white trim, as though they had never been in the light gray of the previous year. The race numbers remained as the year before: number 60 assigned to NX1202; 46 to NX1204. Absorbed in another flying assignment, Mantz had decided to step aside after his three consecutive wins, and assigned the flying of his Mustangs to hired pilots. The race fever was not yet out of Mantz's blood, however, for on the night before the race, he asked each of his two pilots if they would step aside so that he could enter. At the same time, Mantz was aware of the disappointment that each would have felt in not being part of the challenge, so he honored his prior commitment to the pilots.

The start in 1949 was an unusual one. The race was moved to Rosamond Dry Lake, on the Mojave Desert in Southern California, for the sprint to Cleveland. There would be no question about the winner, for a race-horse start was used for the six entries.

Another Mustang, a former F-6C flown by Joe DeBona, won, setting a sky-burning 470.1-mph record for the Bendix. It, too, had been configured with a wet-wing fuel system. Second was number 46, the winner for Mantz the previous year, flown by Stanley Reaver, averaging 450.2 mph. Like the year before, just one mile per hour slower than its sister ship was N1202, flown by Herman "Fish" Salmon. The three Mustangs were followed by a DeHavilland Mosquito, Matin B-26, and a Republic AT-12.

What the entry line-up would have been for the 1950 race has to be left to speculation. The tragic death of Bill Odom in the closed-course Thompson Trophy Race at Cleveland in 1949 is generally blamed for the termination of the National Air Races. In fact, however, it was the start of the Korean Conflict almost ten months later that spelled the end of this event. Part of the former General Motors bomber plant, used as a spectator facility for the races, was returned to military production and could no longer be used for a public event. Other sponsors also withdrew because of wartime commitments.

This also spelled the end of competition racing for the two Mantz P-51Cs, and for months they sat idle, secure in the glory of past victories.

OPPOSITE:
*The namesake of the famous
P-51C* Excalibur III *was the
Vought Sikorsky VS-44. Captain
Blair was not only hired by
American Export Airlines to
fly these majestic flying boats,
but he was with the airplane
from the drawing board, and
was the first to test it for the
company. He stayed with these
airplanes throughout their
operational service. They were
lucky ships for Blair, and he
named his subsequent airplanes
after the first VS-44 that carried the name* Excalibur.

*In 1950 N1202 left the Paul
Mantz stable of airplanes and
was purchased by Capt. Charles
F. Blair, who had plans for
establishing a new round-the-
world speed record. Blair (left)
talks with Paul Penrose, a
renowned Mustang race pilot,
about the capabilities of the
Mustang design. Penrose was
the influencing factor in Blair's
choice of an airplane. (C. F.
Blair)*

New Owner: Charles F. Blair, Jr.

A different type of challenge was soon to be undertaken by NX1202 in the hands of a new owner, and it would part company with its sister ship. That new owner was Charles F. Blair, Jr., an airline captain by profession, and one who had flying conquests of his own to accomplish.

Charlie Blair, a Buffalo-born New Yorker who first flew solo in 1928, studied aeronautical engineering at the University of Michigan and mechanical engineering at the University of Vermont, from which he graduated in 1931. He acquired his Navy wings at Pensacola in 1932, joined Boeing Air Transport (now United Air Lines) in 1933, and in 1940 went with American Export Airlines (AEA) as Chief Pilot, flying the Atlantic to Lisbon. The air route across the Atlantic to Foynes, Ireland, and Lisbon became a main artery to Europe during World War II and AEA's Excalibur flying-boat crossings were of vital importance.

A taste for setting new records may have been whetted for Blair during these transatlantic crossings. Almost by necessity, he set several records while flying the Vought-Sikorsky VS-44 Excaliburs. On his second westbound trip, deteriorating weather at reservicing points kept the flight going to the next stop. As Blair closely watched wind, weather, and fuel, the flight from Foynes, Ireland, extended on to New York City to become the first nonstop airline flight across the Atlantic with passengers and mail. On another eastbound flight in October 1944, with very favorable tailwinds, Blair made the fastest flying-boat crossing of the Atlantic: from New York to Foynes in 14 hours and 17 minutes.

Charlie Blair does not immediately impress one as a man dedicated to setting records. Handsome, soft-spoken, he has a conservative demeanor that conceals the ardent fervor of an idealist. Flying an airliner skillfully, or managing an airline profitably, is only one side of his character. There is another side, which shows more in his work than in his personality: Blair is dedicated, and he is something of a visionary, but if he gives himself a task, he lays it out with precision, and methodically goes through the necessary steps to get it done. Skepticism on the part of others inspires him with greater determination to put his plan into action and make it succeed.

The record for the Atlantic speed crossing that Blair had set had been superseded several times, and the longer he thought about recapturing it, the more it became a workable plan. He would need the right airplane and the best of navigational aids that one man could manage alone. To do this would require considerable capital, and that Blair did not have. He did own an airplane, however, a war-surplus Curtiss C-46 that he leased to others and sometimes operated himself during off time from scheduled airline flying with AEA. The name that Blair had given it was *Excalibur II,* and when he sold it, he had the necessary cash to purchase the airplane with which to set the records he had dreamed of and planned for so carefully.

Charlie Blair was looking for speed and long range in an airplane that he could afford. The winning Mustangs flown by Paul Mantz in the Bendix races would fill two of these prerequisites, but would Mantz sell one—and at a price that Blair could afford?

Mantz was receptive to parting with one of his two Mustangs, selecting N1202 as that aircraft. Blair liked the airplane, and a price of $11,000 was agreed upon, which was to include certain modifications to be made by Mantz

Servicing Diagram P-51 N1202

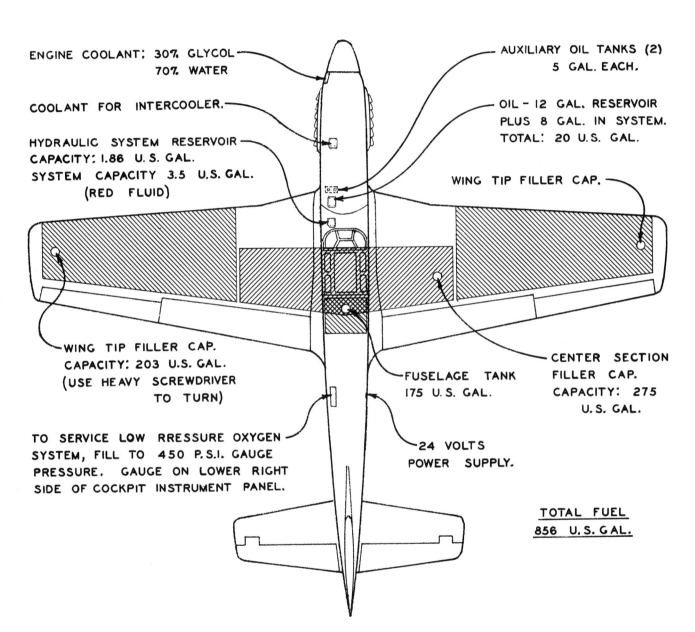

ENGINE COOLANT: 30% GLYCOL 70% WATER

COOLANT FOR INTERCOOLER.

HYDRAULIC SYSTEM RESERVOIR CAPACITY: 1.86 U.S. GAL. SYSTEM CAPACITY 3.5 U.S. GAL. (RED FLUID)

AUXILIARY OIL TANKS (2) 5 GAL. EACH.

OIL - 12 GAL. RESERVOIR PLUS 8 GAL. IN SYSTEM. TOTAL: 20 U.S. GAL.

WING TIP FILLER CAP.

WING TIP FILLER CAP. CAPACITY: 203 U.S. GAL. (USE HEAVY SCREWDRIVER TO TURN)

TO SERVICE LOW RRESSURE OXYGEN SYSTEM, FILL TO 450 P.S.I. GAUGE PRESSURE. GAUGE ON LOWER RIGHT SIDE OF COCKPIT INSTRUMENT PANEL.

FUSELAGE TANK 175 U.S. GAL.

24 VOLTS POWER SUPPLY.

CENTER SECTION FILLER CAP. CAPACITY: 275 U.S. GAL.

TOTAL FUEL 856 U.S. GAL.

NOTE: WING TANKS ARE INTEGRAL TANKS. WHEN TANKS ARE ALMOST FILLED, FUELING IS VERY SLOW. IT IS NECESSARY TO ALLOW FUEL TO SETTLE THROUGHOUT WING, THEN ADDITIONAL FUEL MAY BE ADDED.

before the sale. A new Rolls-Royce Merlin V-1650-9 engine would be installed, replacing the dash-seven he had used in the races. This newer Merlin was known for its rugged reliability, and its two-stage, two-speed supercharger could deliver rated power all the way to 35,000 feet altitude.

The wing was again to be modified for additional fuel capacity, this time by removing the two inboard wing-panel, 85-gallon fuel tanks and sealing that area, thus increasing the capacity to 275 gallons. Mention was made in the letter of agreement by Mantz that the aircraft would then be configured in the same manner as No. 46, his own Mustang. When that modification had taken place, and for what race, is not known.

Other changes included in the sale: replace cracked windows, provide three new tires, and give the Mustang a flashy new coat of wine-red enamel paint.

One of the best P-51 men in the country, according to Mantz, was his superintendent of maintenance, Bob King, and he was made available for the modification project. Work began in early March 1950, and three months later the Mustang was ready for its new owner. The sale was concluded on May 27, 1950, to Associated Air Transport, Inc., of New York, a name that Blair felt was easier to operate under rather than that of a private individual. By July 1, 1950, however, the title was changed to show Charles F. Blair, Jr., as the owner.

Charlie Blair then turned for P-51 information to Paul Penrose, who had been involved in P-51 closed-course racing with the clipped-wing version. Penrose's vivid, authentic description of the remarkable capabilities of this fighter had much to do with Blair's decision to raise his sights from an Atlantic speed-record attempt to a round-the-world project.

Planning for the solo round-the-world flight by Captain Blair was somewhat similar to that of Wiley Post with the *Winnie Mae* in 1933, except that the route would need to detour to the south of Russia. Both pilots recognized the problem of fatigue while flying long distances alone, and installed autopilots. Bill Lear, who was known for his development of the lightweight L-2 autopilot suited for small airplanes, loaned one to Blair and installed it in

For covering the extreme distance that Charles Blair (left) had in mind for his P-51 Mustang, the latest in air navigation equipment was essential. Bill Lear (right), president of Lear Inc., manufacturer of avionics, discusses with Blair the installation of this equipment that was loaned to him for the proposed history-making flight. (C. F. Blair)

the ship. The cockpit became tightly packed with radios and navigation equipment. Radio gear included, among other things, two automatic direction finders, two VHF transmitters and receivers, an HF single-frequency transmitter with trailing wire antenna, and an HF receiver. The two loops for the automatic direction finders were under the coolant airscoops in a single fairing, which broke the standard lines of the Mustang. An emergency radio receiver was installed, operated by dry cells and therefore independent of the ship's electrical system. All the avionics brought the investment up an additional $10,000 over the Mustang's basic purchase price, but Blair was confident that N1202 would meet the task he had set for it.

With the Mustang now under the exclusive care of its new owner, Blair added distinctive markings suited to his own taste. On the sides of the cockpit were painted the American flag, a common practice for airplanes that traversed international borders. For those who knew Charlie Blair, however, this was not so much functional as symbolic of his love of country. White diagonal stripes were added across the tail in a fashion reminiscent of designs used for fighter units during the war. To carry this theme even further, the fighter needed a crest or unit insignia. Not having one, Blair designed one of his own. His imaginative mind captured the weather-vane bird emblem from the top of his home in Port Washington, Long Island, and superimposed the bird in black on a white circle. Little did Blair know that one day a stylized version of this would become the logo of Antilles Air Boats, Inc., the flying-boat service that he would one day operate, as the principal owner, from St. Croix in the U.S. Virgin Islands.

As modifications to his Mustang neared completion and his airline gave a reluctant nod to his proposed solo round-the-world flight, Blair found his plans and the plans of many others changed by the North Koreans, when they invaded South Korea on June 25, 1950. Flying over international borders in a fighter-type airplane in a wartime atmosphere would not be prudent; yet his personal investment in the Mustang was too great to let the airplane sit idle.

After a number of local flights, Blair decided to try N1202's wings in the direction of Alaska. With a few days off from his airline duties that August, Blair pointed the Mustang northward from Los Angeles. The plan was to fly nonstop to Fairbanks for a reasonable shakedown cruise before trying greater things. There was a reason in the back of Charlie Blair's mind for becoming familiar with the approaches at Fairbanks, but more of this later.

This flight did not go as hoped for, and an unscheduled stop was made at Seattle to reevaluate the situation. The engine developed a disconcerting surge that was only relieved when flight altitude was reduced. The autopilot failed to perform satisfactorily, and since there were other aircraft-systems problems to be resolved, it remained inoperative on all the flights. Modifications made to the wing would seem to encourage seeping fuel only along its lower surfaces, and none was expected along the top of the wing. However, low pressure, which creates the lift above the wing, was literally sucking the high octane gasoline from every exposed rivet line along the top surface of the newly prepared wing fuel cavities. This created a disconcerting, volatile mist from across the wing, giving the appearance of a crop duster at work as the Mustang sped through the upper atmosphere. Anxiety lessened when the vapor mist subsided as the fuel level was lowered.

Blair continued the trip to Fairbanks the next morning with a new perspective of coping with the aches and ailments of the reworked airplane.

Pilot and plane became more tolerant of each other, and the remainder of the flight was relatively uneventful.

Fuel seepage persisted, however, and 150 gallons of the precious fuel had drained out overnight at Fairbanks. Despite this and other difficulties, there was little else to do but reservice and fly the airplane as it was. There were no airline connections to Los Angeles that would allow Blair time to meet his flight crew schedule of Pan American's[5] Stratocruiser from New York to London in just a few days. Besides, he could hardly leave his golden nugget at such a far-off location, where repair facilities were limited.

The annoying shortcomings of the Mustang persisted on the flight to Los Angeles, but the trip was made without further incident in eight hours. So unheralded was the plane's arrival that night, that little mention was ever made of the fact that this was the first nonstop flight from Fairbanks, Alaska, to Los Angeles. The record was not important, but finding out the capabilities of this airplane was.

On this shakedown visit to Fairbanks, the name displayed on the nose of

For a short period, N1202 carried the name Stormy Petrel, *a small, long-range bird of the sea, which also was a herald of ill fortune. Blair had many problems at first with the airplane, and superstitious or not, he soon changed the name in hope of better luck with the Mustang.*

5. American Export Airlines (AEA) became American Overseas Airline (AOA) in 1945, owned by American Airlines. Assets of AOA by now had been merged with Pan American.

Ready for his first history-making flight in Excalibur III, *Blair gives a parting wave as he prepares to leave New York's International Airport for the nonstop flight to London. It was a cold, dark morning that January 31, 1951, for the 04:50 EST takeoff. Crossing the Atlantic in an airplane of this size was a rarity, but this craft had the range, and Blair established a new speed record in making the crossing. (Pan American World Airways)*

the Mustang was *Stormy Petrel*. Before long, this was replaced by the more noble-sounding name *Excalibur III*, and Charlie Blair gives a good reason why:

I've never been too superstitious before, but there may be something in a name. A stormy petrel is a small, long-range bird of the sea. It is also reputed to be a herald of ill fortune. Misfortune dogged this airplane while it bore the name. Every flight I made from its original base at Burbank in California produced some mechanical problem that taxed my ingenuity. Some of the difficulties were circumvented by devising odd procedures; others just cost a lot of money, which I was running out of. The new equipment needed more extensive test-flying than had been planned, and this couldn't be left safely undone. Being the lone backer of this project, the bills and the bad luck were on my back. When I started suspecting the name of my airplane, it became time for a change.

Excalibur III *has done better. My other* Excaliburs *were luck ships when I flew them, and I haven't forgotten the story of King Arthur. There was magic in his sword* Excalibur. *Now there is magic in this little airplane.*

A hobby of this proportion had to be productive in some manner, and to recapture the Atlantic crossing speed record for Charlie Blair was *Excalibur III*'s next undertaking. Blair had made 435 crossings by that time, heading the crew of four-engine airliners, but this would be his first crossing alone, and this time he would depend on only one engine.

Excalibur III had been flown to New York in October 1950 to be in readiness for the Atlantic crossing. A three-day break in Blair's airline schedule had been planned for a time when the upper winds were to be the most favorable. It was a bitter cold morning on January 31, 1951, when the lone airman took to the air out of New York International Airport. Takeoff had been set at 02.30 EST, but because of a frozen valve on the refueling truck the departure was not until 04.50. Blair climbed through ice-filled clouds to the fast-flowing river of air called the jet stream.

This phenomenon of high-velocity wind was above the altitude capability of most propeller-driven aircraft, and much was still to be learned in locating this invisible flow of air. Aided by Pan Am's weather forecasters in New York, Blair plotted the best flight path. Cruising altitude varied from 29,000 feet to as high as 37,000 feet. The core of the jet stream was not the guiding force, because its center lay somewhat to the south of the great circle route he had chosen to fly, but the route did intersect the center of the stream in the vicinity of weather ship *Charlie*, which was near the midpoint of the crossing. This gave the needed push with a tail wind estimated at 230 mph, which lasted for several hundred miles east of the weather ship.

The delayed takeoff from New York brought about a night landing at London's smog-shrouded airport. *Excalibur III* touched down at 17.38 London time, 7 hours and 48 minutes after leaving New York. The 3,500-mile, nonstop flight was made at an average speed of 450 mph and broke the old record by 1 hour and 7 minutes. The Merlin functioned perfectly, producing maximum continuous power of 46″ Hg. all the way. No other piston-engine airplane has exceeded that mark, and this record made by Captain Blair and *Excalibur III* may stand indefinitely.

Two days later, Blair was eastbound again across the same route, this time in his routine role as captain of a Pan American Stratocruiser. A passenger stopped him in the aisle and said, "Captain, I hear a Pan Am pilot just flew across here on one engine—all by himself—you know, solo. Must be crazy."

"Must be," replied Blair, typically casual.

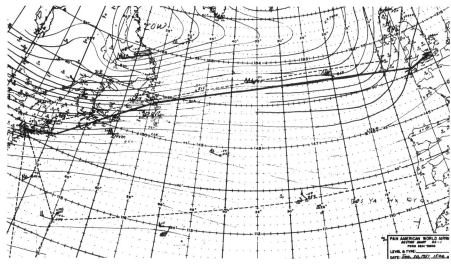

An enthusiastic gathering met the little red airplane piloted by Charles Blair when it arrived at London's Heathrow Airport. A new speed record of 7 hours and 48 minutes for the crossing had been established. This was a transatlantic record for all aircraft at that time, and is still the piston-engine record, which may never be broken. (C. F. Blair)

Winds-aloft chart used by Charles Blair for the Atlantic speed crossing. At near midpoint, the helping winds were giving Excalibur III a ground speed of 600 mph. (C. F. Blair)

Challenge of the Polar Route

Excalibur III remained in England for several months waiting for its master's summer vacation so it could be flown back home. Several routes could be followed, but the challenge of returning via the northern route across the North Pole had been Charlie Blair's plan for a long while.

This was not an easy route, but to explore a means of navigation across this shortest line between Europe and the other side of the world had future merit. The problems of sufficient flying range had been licked, but the major obstacles were the lack of navigational aides across the vastness of the polar icecap, and the fact that magnetic compasses became useless in the northernmost regions of the earth. How he planned to accomplish this flight is best described by Captain Blair:

It is the preparation for a trip of this kind which always proved to be the hardest part of the venture. I was particularly concerned with the navigational problem, of course, and had worked the entire navigational procedure out over and over again to check the possibility of a misconception. I had originally planned the flight almost a year before and had gone over the navigation with American Overseas Airlines Chief Navigator. Several months before the flight I paid a visit to the famous expert navigator, Captain P. V. H. Weems, to get his stamp of approval. Captain Weems wasn't too pleased with my single engine but he indicated that my theory was entirely correct and we sat down and worked out the entire problem backwards and forwards to be sure there were no mistakes. I had selected

Excalibur III had almost four months to wait at London's airport before its owner returned to fly it back to the United States. Pan American, the company for which Blair was a Boeing 377 Stratocruiser Flight Captain, made hangar space available for the airplane during its London stay.

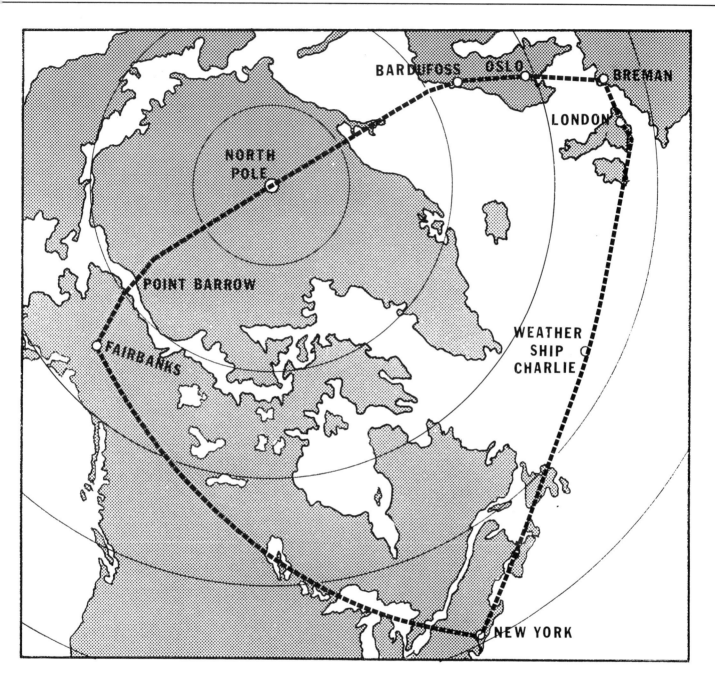

the 29th day of May for the flight across to Alaska because the moon had
a northerly declination on that date and its position was almost 90°
from the sun. As it turned out the presence of the moon was of no
importance, but the fact that it was available in the sky made me feel
better. The 30th of May was selected as an alternative in case of weather
or mechanical problems on the 29th. The departure time from Bardufoss in
Northern Norway was set up for 15.00 GMT and a delayed departure for
16.00. There were four sets of precomputations, two for the 29th and two
for the 30th worked out for the two departure times. The Bardufoss
departure time was set up in mid afternoon for various reasons, one of
them being that the sun bearings at that time were in a convenient position
relative to my astro-compass installation.

  Altitude curves for the sun and moon were plotted, and precomputed fixes

The return of Excalibur III *to the United States via the North Pole was Blair's plan. He took time off from Pan American in the latter part of May 1951, and returned to London to ready his P-51C for the flight. First, he flew the airplane to Hucknall, near Derby, so Rolls-Royce technicians there could peak up the engine. (Rolls-Royce Limited)*

This classic view of a Mustang emphasizes its powerful engine and air-chewing, four-bladed propeller. The over-the-North Pole flight was started here at the airport in Oslo, Norway, where Excalibur III *is shown receiving its final servicing of oxygen from the cart near the tail.*

RIGHT:

The Merlin engine is noted for its smooth-running operation. Rolls Royce personnel gave the engine a complete check at their experimental flying field at Hucknall. Engineers cringed upon seeing the wooden wedges, wires, and tape that secured lines in place, but left them unaltered because of the success they had achieved. (Rolls-Royce Limited)

for the sun and moon for a given time were spotted all over the chart midway between the Pole and Point Barrow. All I had to do was raise my Link sextant and look at my watch. Because of the cramped quarters it wasn't practical to rummage around in the tables for the answer.

Most important of all, sun azimuths were plotted for each hour. As it actually turned out the trip could have been flown very successfully using nothing more than these azimuths of the sun, and Point Barrow radio.

This summarizes the navigational problem as it was considered one month before the flight was scheduled to take off. Blair's vacation time from the airline arrived in mid-May, and he set off to rejoin *Excalibur III* in London. Pan American World Airways in London and Rolls-Royce at Hucknall put the ship, engine, and radio in top condition, and in late May plane and pilot flew to Oslo, which was to be the starting point for the trip to New York. The payload for the flight across the top of the world would be 3,000 covers of Norwegian mail to be auctioned off for the Damon Runyon Cancer Fund.

The flight to Oslo provided the final functional check of accessories and equipment before the long leap. In Oslo the Norwegian Royal Air Force (NRAF), the Norwegian Civil Aeronautics Association (CAA), and the weather forecasters at the Norwegian Meteorological Institute offered Blair their enthusiastic help. The NRAF dispatched a Catalina flying boat to patrol to the south of Spitzbergen and maintain radio contact as long as possible. The CAA arranged for all radio beacons in northern Norway and Spitzbergen to be functioning when *Excalibur III* was in their vicinity. The weather information from the Pole south to Fairbanks was to be furnished by Pan American in collaboration with the U.S. Air Force in Alaska, to be teletyped to Oslo.

Everything worked out as planned, and late in the morning of May 29, 1951, *Excalibur III* proceeded to Bardufoss near Tromsoe, Norway, which lies slightly to the north of the Arctic Circle. The only mishap of the entire

RIGHT:

Captain Blair makes one final check of his astro compass before leaving Oslo, as a Pan Am mechanic assists. The basic navigational equipment needed for this polar crossing was relatively simple and inexpensive, but the major success of the mission was based upon flawless, predetermined calculations for specific points and time.

Giving a parting wave to those assisting him at Oslo, Captain Blair settles into the cockpit of Excalibur III *for the first leg to Bardufoss, Norway, for this history-making flight of May 29, 1951.*

RIGHT:

While Blair circled to land at Bardufoss, Norway, the northernmost jumping-off point for the polar flight, the right rear cockpit cover parted company with Excalibur III. *It was soon re-covered; Royal Norwegian Air Force men are busy here preparing to reattach it. Captain Blair (left) discusses his departure plans with the commanding officer of the RNAF fighter outpost, Lt. Col. Jon Tvedte, right. (C. F. Blair)*

The wing tip was an odd location for a P-51C to be serviced with fuel, but this airplane was a special case. The entire wing was modified to hold gasoline, 681 gallons in all, plus 175 gallons in a fuselage tank behind the pilot's seat. Tanks were topped off at Bardufoss for the long journey to Fairbanks, Alaska. (C. F. Blair)

There was some concern about the tail wheel on Excalibur III. Corrosion was noticed, and the load placed upon it was excessive because of the over-sized aft fuselage tank and more wing fuel aft of the main landing gear. Note the patched seams along the top of the wing, where, on a flight the year before, the low pressure above the wing had literally sucked fuel out through these fine skin openings. (C. F. Blair)

RIGHT:

The loneliness that this only occupant of Excalibur III was to experience over the frozen north already seems in evidence in this picture of Charlie Blair as he makes a final check of the few objects that he can take with him. Onlookers seem very intent on the airplane. (C. F. Blair)

trip occurred while Blair circled to land at this small strip built by the Germans during World War II. The right cockpit enclosure behind the folding canopy came loose, glanced off the stabilizer, and fell in the vicinity of the field. Spectators saw this falling object, recovered it, and reinstalled it for the American flier. It remained securely attached for the rest of the flight.

After a three-hour stay at Bardufoss, for refueling, minor maintenance, and a visual check of the runway down which the overloaded, tail-heavy Mustang would depart, all seemed in readiness. At 14.58 GMT on May 29, 1951, the historic flight to Fairbanks via the North Pole was on its way. The pilot, who remained wedged in the confining cockpit of *Excalibur III* for this unprecedented flight, briefly relates the event as it happened:

I had one radio contact with the RNAF flying boat near Spitzbergen and got excellent ADF bearings on Bear Island and Svalbard radio station, the latter radio facility being on Spitzbergen. At Spitzbergen I climbed to 22,000 feet, cruising at 325 miles an hour correcting my course slightly for a forecasted westerly wind. I was on top of all clouds, but the cloud deck had been solid over Spitzbergen so I did not see the island. I changed my astro-compass setting approximately two degrees every ten minutes and took an occasional shot at the sun which showed that I was holding course very nicely.

Hours passed by and the Merlin is running without a trace of roughness. If it should fail, there would be no choice but to ride the airplane down to whatever kind of landing the surface might afford. It would be futile to bail out and leave behind the survival gear which could not be attached to my parachute. Outside, the temperature at 22,000 feet was minus 25 degrees Centigrade. Basking in the cockpit heated by the Merlin engine I felt no discomfort in my light-weight summer flying suit.

The sextant was preset for the sun's declination. At 19.55 GMT according to my reckoning, Excalibur III should be crossing the top of the world. When the time reached 19.55 GMT, I pointed the sextant at the sun. The little green pea of the sun wobbles once again in the center of the bubble. Suddenly I'm heading due south. The sensation of reaching a long-sought

35

A last-minute check is made by Blair of his oxygen mask and helmet. Clothing was light and loose-fitting, more than adequate in the tightly enclosed cockpit warmed by the Merlin engine. Should he have been forced down in the far off northern reaches of the world, chances of survival for any length of time, even with heavier clothing, would have been remote. (C. F. Blair)

RIGHT:
Charles Blair makes last-minute seat and parachute strap adjustments before climbing into Excalibur III. He would be sitting for a long time in one position, and twisted or out-of-place seat straps could become very uncomfortable. Every corner of the cockpit was filled with extra equipment; it was obvious that this fighter was not designed for a big pilot. (C. F. Blair)

RIGHT:
The time had come for the scheduled departure. Captain Blair is secured in the tiny cockpit of Excalibur III, and onlookers wait expectantly for the first turn of the propeller as the Mustang is about to come alive. (C. F. Blair)

Excalibur III warms up at the chocks at this northernmost airfield on the mainland of Norway. With a parting wave to those standing by, who had become close friends in the few short hours during preparation, Blair prepares to take off. It was a difficult departure in a sense, in the face of the dangers that lay ahead. (C. F. Blair)

With the engine barely ticking over, the little red Mustang taxies out for takeoff after a three-hour stay at Bardufoss. At 14.58 GMT, two minutes ahead of Blair's projected first takeoff calculations, Excalibur III was airborne for the long, lonely journey. So far everything was working without a hitch, and because of the careful planning of every detail, the flight continued to go smoothly. (C. F. Blair)

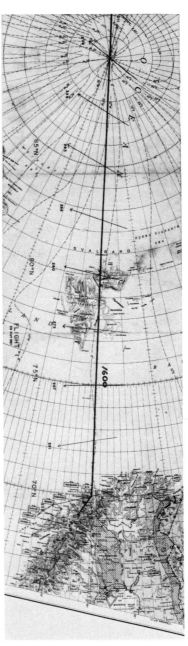

This is the map prepared by Captain Blair for his polar flight. A slight dog-leg at the beginning of the flight placed Excalibur III on the 20th east meridian for his route to the North Pole. The arrows across the route of flight are precomputed positions for every 150 nautical miles and equaled 30 minutes of flying time, showing the relative bearing off the nose for the sun vector. By altering the heading of the airplane to achieve these bearings, Blair held Excalibur III on course. (C. F. Blair)

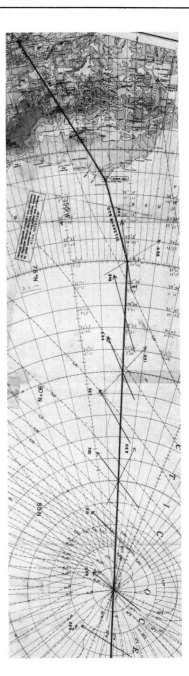

Excalibur III crossed the North Pole at 19.55 GMT on May 29, 1951. At that point, every direction was south. Sunline bearings began moving to the nose position, as shown by their plots on the map. Arrows to the right were for taking fixes from the moon, but because of haze, the moon was not seen, nor needed. At the 75th north parallel, southbound, the course departed the 160th west meridian and was altered to the left to home-in on the radio beacon at Point Barrow, Alaska, then on to Fairbanks. (C. F. Blair)

"FRM FBKO QUOTE BLAIR JUST OVER FIELD MAKING APPROACH NOW
NO RADIO CONTACT AT ALL ON HIM INQUOTE." CEBFI 300131Z

There was no communication with Blair after he left the other side of the world. Many waited anxiously through the more than ten hours for word from Excalibur III. This simple message from Fairbanks, relayed to Blair's wife, brought an end to the suspense that was felt during the anxious hours.

The arrival of Excalibur III *at New York was exciting. Newsmen were at hand for this historic moment when the airplane returned—the hard way—to its starting point from Europe. The Boeing Stratocruiser in the background was the type of aircraft that Blair routinely flew to and from Europe, but over a more conventional route. (C. F. Blair)*

goal was fleeting—over before I realized it had happened. I was robbed of the chance to savor it.

After passing the Pole the haze even further restricted the visibility. Because of this haze condition the moon never put in an appearance, which disturbed me slightly, but not enough to cause me to climb above the haze although I did climb to cruise at 25,000 feet at 85 degrees North on the southward run. At 80 degrees North I pick up the station at Point Barrow on my ADF and crossed it with a sun-line, which showed me to be exactly where I thought I was. This pleased me to no end, and I crossed the Coast of Alaska at Point Barrow one minute ahead of flight plan. I had never seen the moon and am now convinced that the moon is of little importance to a fast aircraft. I landed at Fairbanks one hour and forty minutes after passing Barrow.

Oddly enough, I arrived in Fairbanks a half hour before my departure at Bardufoss, on the same day, thus gaining on the clock. My flight time was 10 hours 27 minutes bucking an average 10-knot headwind.

This was a heady moment in an hour of triumph. But it was a fleeting moment. The action that leads to victory—leaves the more indelible recollections.

Ten hours after their arrival at Fairbanks, Blair and *Excalibur III* departed nonstop for New York, via the airways, a distance of 3,450 miles. This was another cross-country sprint—seemingly a way of life for *Excalibur III* that started five years before at the Bendix Transcontinental Air Races.

38

Excalibur III *comes to rest at the terminal in New York after its flight from Fairbanks. Another record had just been added to the growing list for this record-setting P-51C. This was the first transcontinental solo nonstop flight connecting Fairbanks and New York. The polar flight that preceded it rightfully received much more acclaim. (C. F. Blair)*

OPPOSITE, BOTTOM:
The first airmail to cross the North Pole was carried on board this flight of Excalibur III. *Upon arriving at New York, Charlie Blair hands a mail sack containing 3,000 commemorative postcards to Ernie Kehr, American Airmail Service vice president. (Pan American World Airways)*

The trip would be her last, yet one that would end as another milestone in aviation history. This was the first transcontinental solo flight across this Alaska-Canadian route, nonstop between Fairbanks and New York. Flight time to Idlewild Airport was 9½ hours at normal cruise speed, for there was no speed record to be broken on this route.

All the difficulties and problems encountered by Charlie Blair on his polar flight cannot be covered in a story of this length. With technology and its related high costs going beyond the capabilities of any one man, Charles F. Blair, Jr., may well be the last aviation pioneer to achieve his goals unaided by team effort. When most record attempts are made, a number of people join in a team, ranging from skilled engineers, coordinators, and plane handlers at stopover points. Although Captain Blair had sanctuary and assistance at several Pan American World Airways facilities, and fuel was supplied by Pan Am for the flight from Europe to Alaska and New York, he himself was responsible for every detail and all the financing of these flights. None of his accomplishments were in the spirit of exhibitionism, but rather in the spirit of development and progress for the aviation industry. There was no prize money or bonus check waiting at the other end of his air routes as incentive. Surprise that it was, the award of the Harmon International Trophy in 1952 by the President of United States was the best tribute possible for Blair's accomplishments for the previous year in the field of aviation.

On November 18, 1952, in the Oval Office of the White House, Captain

Tired from his flight, but pleased with his accomplishment after returning to New York, Charlie Blair rests a moment before leaving the cramped confines of the cockpit of Excalibur III. (C. F. Blair)

Three thousand of these commemorative postcards were carried on board Excalibur III and became the first official transpolar covers. This was not the first time that covers were flown over the top of the world, but it was the first time that covers were regarded as "airmail" in the full sense of the word. The first transpolar souvenir covers were those carried by Amundsen, Ellsworth, and Nobile aboard the Norge airship between Kings Bay, Spitsbergen, and Teller, Alaska, where the dirigible was forced down before reaching its destination, in April 1926. The previous year Amundsen and Ellsworth had flown from Kings Bay to the North Pole and back. On both trips covers were taken, and while they were postmarked by courtesy of postal clerks, they were not considered as "mail" by postal authorities. They are listed in the "American Air Mail Catalogue" as "semi-official." The Blair souvenirs represent a double-record flight because he broke existing aviation records between Norway and Alaska, and between Fairbanks and New York. These cards were later sold for a dollar or more donation to aid the Damon Runyon Cancer Fund, which was very active in the forties and fifties.

For his accomplishment in being the first to fly a single-engine fighter plane nonstop across the North Pole from Norway to Alaska, Capt. Charles F. Blair, Jr., was presented the Harmon International Trophy on November 18, 1952, by President Harry S Truman. Blair's development of a simplified, "prepackaged," long-range celestial navigation technique for such a flight was a significant contribution to aviation, and justified this recognition and award. Looking on is Navy Lt. Comdr. Carl J. Seiberlich, who was honored for his advancements in antisubmarine warfare equipment. (Pan American World Airways)

Excalibur III had fulfilled its purpose, and its flying days were over. Charlie Blair makes a final check of the cockpit as the airplane is prepared for disassembly at Pan American's facility at LaGuardia Airport. (Pan American World Airways)

Blair received this highly honored trophy from President Harry S Truman. The citation accompanying it reads as follows:

To Captain Charles F. Blair, Jr., in recognition of being the first to fly a single-engine fighter plane, nonstop across the North Pole from Norway to Alaska by means of a new streamlined "pre-packaged" long range celestial navigation technique for high speed aircraft on 29 May 1951.

| The White House Washington, D.C. | Presented by: Harry S Truman President, United States of America |

Excalibur III had more than met the challenges for which Captain Blair had acquired this Mustang—and offers were plentiful from would-be buyers for the airplane. But for Charlie Blair, there was only one rightful place for this historic craft with so many achievements, and that was with the Aeronautical Collection of the Smithsonian Institution in Washington, D.C. The Smithsonian accepted his offer, but a donation representing a life savings needed further thought by the plane's owner.

Fortunately, officials at Pan American World Airways recognized the accomplishments performed by one of their senior pilots, and agreed to purchase *Excalibur III* for a token price of $10,000, Blair's initial investment, for presentation of the aircraft to the museum.

The fuselage of Excalibur III is separated from its wing as Captain Blair, in his Pan American uniform, looks on during a break in his scheduled airline flights. His sentimental attachment to this airplane is understandable, considering his accomplishments in the plane. (Pan American World Airways)

The handling of disassembled components of an airplane is a difficult task. Specially made jigs and support frames are necessary to handle the unruly components that no longer balance at normal lift points as they did when the aircraft was fully assembled. (Pan American World Airways)

Snugly packed aboard a flat-bed trailer, Excalibur III *leaves LaGuardia for storage at Reading, Pennsylvania, to await delivery to the National Air Museum in Washington, D.C. (Pan American World Airways)*

Pan American World Airways System

requests the pleasure of your company

at the presentation to the National Air Museum

of the first solo trans-polar airplane

piloted by Captain Charles F. Blair, Jr.

from Norway to Alaska on May 29, 1951

Friday afternoon the sixth of November

Nineteen hundred and fifty-three

at four o'clock

The Smithsonian Institution

After the flight from Alaska to Idlewild, the P-51 had been flown across the Hudson River to Teterboro Airport, New Jersey, a few days later—one of this airplane's few nonrecord-setting flights. There it remained hangared for about eleven months while its fate was being decided. When negotiations with Pan Am were concluded, Blair again flew *Excalibur III* for the short, and this time final, flight to LaGuardia Airport where Pan Am took ownership on May 29, 1952. This transfer took place just one year to the day after the historic polar flight. Work began almost immediately to disassemble the airplane so that it could be placed aboard a truck bed. On June 4, the Mustang reached Reading, Pennsylvania, where it remained in a hangar until the Smithsonian was able to receive it.

A place was created for *Excalibur III* in the old metal building of the National Air Museum for the presentation and public exhibit. At formal ceremonies on November 6, 1953, *Excalibur III* joined the ever-increasing list of aircraft, both technical and historical, which millions of visitors a year see and admire. This recognition is a fitting reward for *Excalibur III*, and a lasting tribute to the men who flew her.

A relatively large number of the more popular bubble-canopied P-51Ds survive throughout the world. Except for two or three less than complete aircraft, of the 3,738 earlier-type P-51Bs and Cs—not including F-6s and A-36s—only two complete specimens exist in museums today, both being Cs purchased originally by Paul Mantz. These are N1202, *Excalibur III*, at the National Air and Space Museum, and NX1204, which after Mantz's death passed to the ownership of Frank Tallman and is on exhibit at the International Flight and Space Museum at Orange County Airport, Santa Ana, California. Both Mustangs were originally registered by Mantz on August 9, 1946, along with a third aircraft, a North American B-25 with registration number NX1203. Mantz converted this B-25 Mitchell for special motion picture photo work. It crashed in 1976.

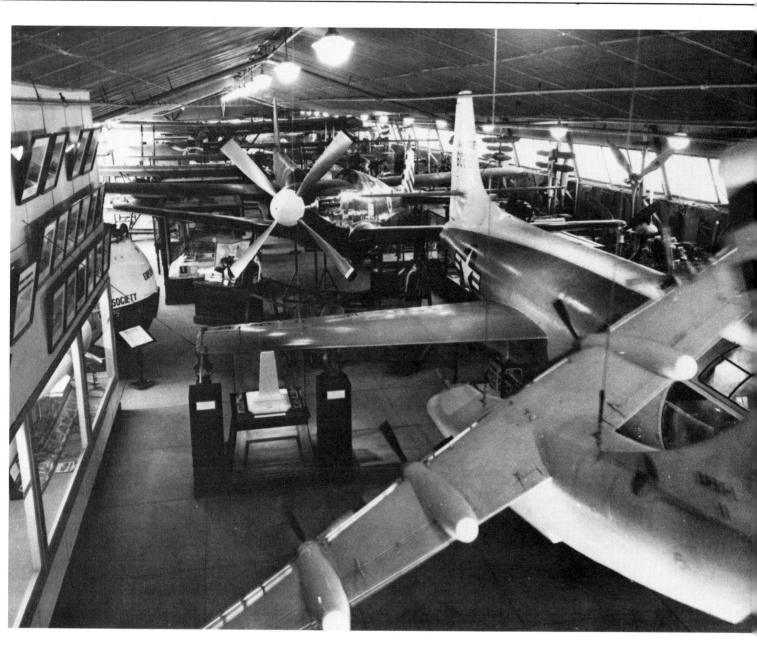

LEFT:

Excalibur III *stands in a well-deserved place of honor. Inside the metal building of the National Air Museum on November 6, 1953, Charles Blair makes the presentation of Excalibur III on behalf of Pan American World Airways System. Receiving the aircraft is Dr. Leonard Carmichael, Secretary of the Smithsonian Institution.*

The massive four-bladed propeller of Excalibur III *stands out prominently among the cramped exhibits in the metal building of the National Air Museum of the 1950s. This building was noted for its abundance of airplanes in a limited space. In the foreground is a radio-controlled flying model of the Convair XP5Y-1 Tradewind, followed by the Bell X-1 research aircraft, the first airplane to fly faster than the speed of sound. Behind* Excalibur III *are other famous aircraft, such as the XP-59, Douglas World Cruiser, and many more.*

44

Marking schemes carried by

N1202

A Dallas-built North American
P-51C in the markings that the
subject airplane would have
carried when first delivered to
the U.S. Army Air Force.

B NX1202 appeared for the 1946
Bendix Race in Paul Mantz Air
Service colors of bright red and
white trim. A special dorsal fin
was added.

C For establishing a new transcontinental speed record,
NX1202 carried the name Blaze
of Noon in water-soluble paint
that also covered race number 46.

D The marking scheme for the
1947 Bendix Race was identical
to that of the previous year.
The rear window was painted
over to conceal the larger fuselage fuel tank. A Bendix ADF
loop in housing on airscoop was
added.

E For the 1948 Bendix Race,
N1202 carried the Flying
Shamrock colors. The airplane
was light gray with shamrock
and marking details in kelly
green. Spinner, wing, and tail
tips were red. The race number
was changed to 60.

F Returning again to bright red
as in the first two race years,
N1202 retained race number 60
of the previous year. The rudder
was now solid red.

G Final markings and color for
N1202 consisted of a darker red
for its last owner, Capt. Charles
F. Blair. A double-loop antenna
was housed in a larger fairing.
For a brief time the airplane
carried the name Stormy Petrel,
but this was changed to Excalibur III for its history-making
flights with Blair.

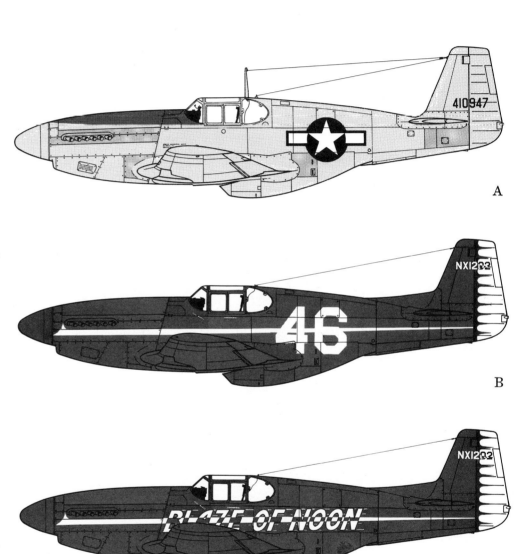

A

B

C

D

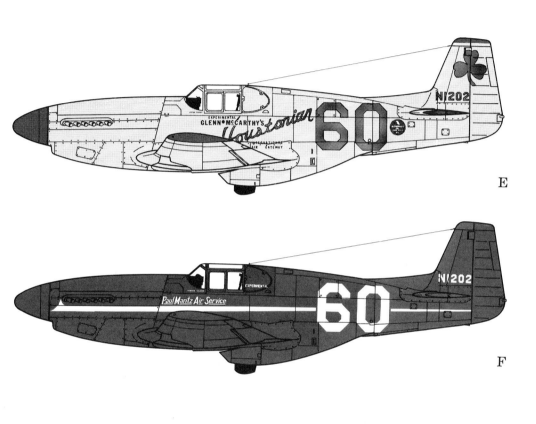

E

F

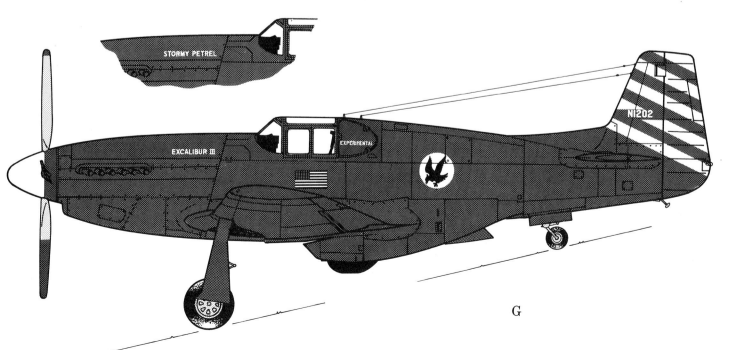

G

A little-known fact about NX1204, Excalibur III's racing sister ship, is revealed by this color photo that shows its fuselage painted yellow for the 1947 Bendix Transcontinental Race, a change from its unpainted condition of the previous year. (Bill Greeley)

RIGHT:
Somewhat faded with time, this color picture of N1202 shows the Mustang at Van Nuys, California, for the start of the 1946 Bendix Race. (Dustin W. Carter)

NX1204 is now at the International
Flight and Space Museum in Santa
Ana, California. This picture was
taken in the 1960s at Orange County
Airport. (Dustin W. Carter)

RIGHT:
An exuberant crowd greets
Excalibur III, piloted by Captain
Charles Blair, for the afternoon
arrival on May 30, 1951, at New
York International Airport. This
arrival from Fairbanks, Alaska, was
the final leg of the history-making
flight across the top of the world,
Norway to Alaska. (C. F. Blair)

The barber-pole tail of Excalibur III is the distinguishing mark for this demilitarized P-51C. The photograph was taken in October 1977 at the end of the Mustang's detailed restoration.

RIGHT:
Symbolic of P-51 design is the large four-bladed propeller driven by the reliable and powerful V-1650 Merlin engine.

ABOVE, LEFT:
The cockpit of Excalibur III *appears confining, but access to controls and instruments are within easy reach of the pilot.*

ABOVE, RIGHT:
With the installation of the restored Merlin engine in the fuselage of Excalibur III, *Walter Roderick and Joseph Fichera see that all lines and controls are connected as if the aircraft were to be flown.*

LEFT CENTER:
This view shows the left side of the cockpit, which contains the throttle quadrant, trim, landing gear, and wing-flap controls.

LEFT BOTTOM:
The right side of the cockpit has mostly electrical controls and radio equipment.

In September 1977 Excalibur III once again resembled an airplane as it neared the final phase of its restoration. Removed from exhibit in the late 1950s, it remained disassembled while in storage over the years. This is Building 10 at Silver Hill, Maryland, where NASM restorations take place.

When restoration of Excalibur III resumed in 1976, only the rudder counterbalance weight retained a sufficient area of the original aircraft paint to analyze and record. Sanding through the various layers of paint confirmed much of the history of this P-51C. These colors coincided with the sequence of events for this historic airplane, and gave evidence of the color shades that were used.

Color surfaces for N1202 (Munsell color code equivalents):
1. *White—tail stripe*
2. *Dark red 2.5R 2/6—overall finish*
3. *Red 7.5 4/10—1949 overall finish*
4. *Kelly green 5G 4/6—shamrock for 1948 race*
5. *Light gray N 6.5/—1948 overall finish*
6. *Medium gray primer surfacer*
7. *Red 7.5R 4/10—1947 overall finish*
8. *Medium gray primer surfacer*
9. *Red 7.5R 4/10—1946 overall finish*
10. *Medium gray primer surfacer N 3.5/*
11. *Zinc chromate*
12. *Bare metal*

II Restoring "Excalibur III"

In 1962 Excalibur III *was removed from short-duration storage and moved to Building 10 at the museum's facility for restoration. The fuselage of this P-51C is shown here just before its paint was removed for corrosion control of its metal structure and skin covering.*

The question most often asked about newly restored aircraft of the National Air and Space Museum is: *can the airplane be flown?* The answer generally warrants both a "yes" and a "no" response, and therefore requires further explanation. For *Excalibur III,* whose restoration was completed in October 1977, the question of its airworthiness also requires this ambiguous reply.

Qualifying for the "yes" response, *Excalibur III* is complete, with all its internal components restored and installed for its various hydraulic, electrical, and mechanical systems. In theory, everything needed for flight is in place. Flight controls are connected, and the structure was fully inspected for corrosion and damage. Any defects that were discovered were repaired with expert craftsmanship. Quite often, this attention exceeds that required for aircraft intended to be flown.

For the "no" answer, it must be remembered that aircraft of the National Aeronautical Collection are preserved during the restoration process to ensure the longest possible life as a museum artifact. To prepare them in this way requires some processes that do not lead toward airworthiness. One example of this occurs in the processing of the engine. Although the engine is complete in every detail, the interior walls are coated with a protective film to guard against rust and corrosion. This is not conducive to a well-running engine! This material could be removed, however, if the engine had to be made operational again. During restoration, aircraft systems, such as hydraulic, fuel, and electrical, are not checked for operation. Many seals and valves would not withstand system pressures, and some electrical components would have to be replaced because of their age. With such replacement, however, the original parts would be lost, and with them the record of the

51

original technology. A museum airplane best serves its purpose as a static specimen for study, rather than as a flyable example, subject to damage, and possible total destruction. Therefore, the National Air and Space Museum (NASM) has a rigid policy that its aircraft will not be flown.

No two restorations of National Aeronautical Collection aircraft are alike. Each has its separate points of technological interest, as well as its individual problems. This description of the restoration of *Excalibur III* has two purposes: (1) to continue the recording of the history of this famous airplane of which its restoration is a vital part and (2) to assist others who may have similar restoration projects, by outlining the methods of accomplishing this work and providing an idea of the time, cost, and problems encountered.

The restoration of *Excalibur III* stretched over many years, with long interludes of inactivity. Following its removal from exhibit in 1958 or 1959 from what was called the "old tin building" of the National Air Museum on Independence Avenue in Washington, it was moved to Silver Hill, Maryland, where the museum's Preservation and Restoration Facility is located. After a brief period of storage, this P-51C was selected for restoration, and work first began on April 13, 1962. *Excalibur III* was showing the wear of time, and it was to be readied like so many other aircraft for future exhibit in the proposed new building of the National Air and Space Museum.

Wing Restoration
a Major Problem

Before outlining the various restoration processes used for *Excalibur III*, many of which can be used for other aircraft, I should discuss the unique trauma encountered with the wing of this P-51C, which developed into a story in itself. What made this wing restoration more difficult than others was its extensive corrosion caused by its unorthodox modification into a wet-wing configuration.

It did not take much handling of the wing to detect the fact that portions of the skin were crumbling. Where the rubberized tank sealer that had been sprayed on the interior of the wing had come loose, fuel and water had become trapped underneath. With the passing of time, considerable corrosion had developed and spread from this trapped moisture on the wing structure and skin.

While this problem was being studied, restoration work ended when a major warehousing project at Silver Hill took priority. By July 23, 1963, 1,391.5 man-hours had been expended on the restoration of *Excalibur III*, and the disassembled parts were moved into a museum warehouse until work could be resumed.

The former owner's interest in this airplane had not ended with its presentation to the museum. Capt. Charles Blair was aware of the disruption in the restoration of *Excalibur III*, and wished to assist with the project. When S. Paul Johnson, the museum's director, agreed to his proposal of outside help, Blair took the problem to Pan American World Airways administrators. (Blair, as noted earlier, was a Flight Captain with the company, and Pan Am had sponsored the donation of *Excalibur III* to the museum.) On July 8, 1965, three supervisors of Pan Am's repair facility at nearby Dulles International Airport inspected the wing. The first plan was that Pan Am would do the structural repair, but after closer inspection the supervisors' estimate of the effort required to repair the corrosion damage was most discouraging, and they recommended that a replacement wing be used.

This thought had been considered during earlier attempts to restore this

The wing of this P-51C suffered the greatest amount of corrosion damage. The photograph at left shows interior damage that was found when sections of skin were removed. A similar area of the wing is shown at right, ready to be reskinned after internal repairs were made. Internally exposed metal surfaces are either painted or clearcoated, depending on the original coatings, to prevent further corrosion.

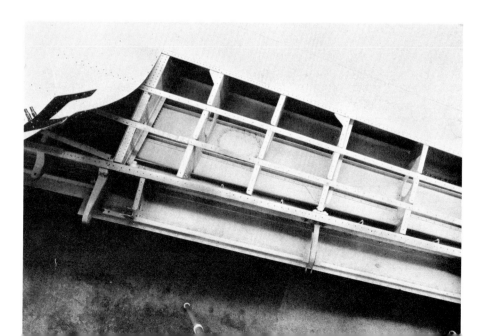

Photographs were taken of all marking details so they could be replaced in the final restoration. Measuring scales were taped in place for these photos as reference guides. This is the tail fin of Excalibur III.

wing by Louis S. Casey, museum curator, and efforts were again directed in that direction. A wing for a P-51C was by then a rare item, but one was located in September 1965 at Pioneer Aero Service, Burbank, California, priced at $3,000. This amount was not only out of the reach of the museum's limited budget, but also another very important factor was involved, one that would detract from the technical significance of the airplane: the unique structural features of *Excalibur III* were the modifications made to the fuel system in the form of the wet wing. With a replacement stock wing, the airplane's internal individuality would be lost.

This was a perplexing problem, which continued to drag on. Charlie Blair was sympathetic toward retaining the original wing, and offered another solution. In addition to his position with Pan American, he operated a commuter air service, Antilles Air Boats, Inc., in the U.S. Virgin Islands. In mid-1966 he proposed sending one or two of his airframe technicians to the museum's facility at Silver Hill to work there on the wing of *Excalibur III*. This plan did not materialize, but in June 1971 a more workable arrangement developed.

Major work for the aircraft of Antilles Air Boats was done by K.C. Aircraft Sheet Metal Company, at Long Beach, California. If NASM would transport the wing to and from that facility, Blair would have the company repair the wing. This was agreed on, and the wing was trucked to California for repairs. The cost to Captain Blair for this work on his former "little red airplane" came to $1,750. When the wing was completed several months later, it was flown back to Silver Hill, space available, on board an Air Force Reserve C-124, and unloaded at nearby Andrews Air Force Base.

What seemed like the end of the problem, however, was just the beginning. The mere handling of the wing in the moving process again caused crumbling of corroded skin areas that had not been detected while the airplane was being worked on in California. Once more, the restoration of *Excalibur III* became dormant.

Too much was at stake for Charlie Blair to let *Excalibur III* wither away as so many disjointed airplane parts. He visited the restoration facility at Silver Hill in November 1973 to see what could be done. At his suggestion, bids were obtained from airframe repair companies in the local area. Of the three bids requested, the most complete proposal—though not the lowest—was submitted by CNC Industries, located at Hyde Field, near Clinton, Maryland. The cost, to be paid by Captain Blair, would be $1,885 for replacing damaged skin areas that showed signs of additional interior corrosion. During this process, technicians from Silver Hill would chemically treat the original wing structure to arrest further corrosion.

As the wing was opened for repair, damage to still other areas, not previously considered for replacement, became evident. To continue the existing contract seemed useless in light of these discoveries. To assure no further skin problems, $1,500 of additional contracted work would be required, and reassurance was given that this would end all skin break-through problems once and for all. Captain Blair again agreed to this additional cost, which now totaled $5,135, and the work continued. When this was accomplished, nearly 50 percent of the original wing skin had been replaced, all because of internal corrosion. The wing was returned to Silver Hill on November 15, 1974, and all seemed in readiness for the future restoration schedule.

"Curatorial Package"

When the workload pressure of opening the new building of the National Air and Space Museum ended on July 1, 1976, a follow-on program of aircraft restoration was undertaken. First on the priority list was the partially completed *Excalibur III,* and its components were brought into Building 10 for restoration at Silver Hill. Heading the work force on the airplane was Reid Ferguson, a senior technician at the museum facility. Work got under way on October 8, 1976.

For any aircraft restoration of this type, a thorough preplanning of the work to be accomplished is essential. The curator in charge of restorations prepares what is called a "Curatorial Package" as the overall plan for the project. This describes the final configuration for the airplane, areas of preservation needing special attention, technical data within the structure to be recorded, and any reconfiguration of the structure that will be necessary for historical technical exactness. Markings and precise colors, along with technical drawings and reference photographs, complete the "Curatorial Package." Copies of this package, in the hands of all persons associated with the restoration, serve as a common plan for all to follow.

Six basic component breakdown headings serve as references for man-hour and cost accounting. These are: *wing, fuselage, cockpit, empennage, engine,* and *finish and assembly.* One of the more important reasons for keeping records of this type is for planning future restorations. The most underestimated aspect of any restoration is the number of man-hours programmed for the task. As the data bank containing records on man-hours expended on various aircraft components increases, a more accurate estimate can be made for future restorations, which will aid work scheduling.

Preparing the Structure

Since *Excalibur III* was to be restored to the configuration in which it was received, the first operation was to make a record of all external markings. This was done by taking a series of photographs of these details with measuring scales placed alongside. In addition and of greater value, pencil tracings of tissue paper were made of the marking designs, with structural reference points included, so they could be reapplied in their original locations.

With the wing separated from the fuselage, engine removed, and tail surfaces detached, the airframe was readied for paint removal. Plexiglass windows were masked and vital openings sealed so that paint remover would not cause damage to these areas. The paint remover was sprayed on and allowed to set for approximately fifteen to thirty minutes before the surface was brushed and the paint loosened with a plexiglass scraper; then the paint was washed off with a stream of water. A hand wiping of the air frame followed, with MEK (methyl-ethyl ketone), to clean around rivet heads and along skin-mating lines. It is very important to remove every trace of paint remover from every crevice, so it will not harm the metal.

Further preparation of the aluminum skin and structure was required. Chemical treatment of all surfaces was done for corrosion protection and to

In addition to the reference photographs of the insignia of Excalibur III, *tissue paper tracings were made for use in final repainting.*

Confirming the original military identity of Excalibur III, *the U.S. Army serial number 44-10947 and P-51C-10-NT-GA and other original data stenciled on the fuselage were photographed as the old layers of paint were removed.*

Much of the skin repair of the wing was done by commercial contractors, sponsored by Excalibur III's former owner, Captain Blair. When work was resumed by the museum, considerable additional corrosion was found in the interior structure, and many portions of the wing had to be opened again.

This comparison photograph, taken in December 1976, shows one wheel well before restoration (foreground) and one nearing completion. Many of the interior details have already been removed from the nearest wheel well. Only one is worked on at a time so that the other can be used as a pattern for replacing parts.

RIGHT:

This closeup view of the completed wheel well shows the many parts and details that are contained inside.

serve as a base for the paint finish. Heavily corroded areas were rubbed with fine aluminum wool or brushed with an aluminum wire brush. Zinc chromate primer was then applied.

More Work on the Wing

There was still additional work to be done on the wing in the normal course of restoration that was not included or intended to be accomplished on the contracted work done outside the museum facility. Basically, this involved the removal of the landing gears for their individual restoration and the reworking of the complex wheel-well areas. It was at this point that a chain of complications with the wing set in again.

Up to then, wing restoration efforts were directed primarily to replacing areas of corroded skin that were evident from the outside, or areas that might cause future problems. Inspection now showed that the large magnesium landing-gear attachment castings were corroded to the point that their wing attachment flanges had been weakened considerably. To completely arrest this corrosion and make suitable repairs, these castings had to be removed from the structure—no simple task since they were attached as one of the strong points of the wing. Once the castings were removed, it was deemed more practical to replace them if better ones could be found. Fortunately, it was possible to obtain such a set from a private owner of P-51 parts in Connecticut. The attachment ears, to which the landing-gear fairing doors were hinged, had been broken from these replacement castings, and those from the former set had to be cut free and welded in their place. This operation required 170 hours of milling, jigging, and welding, in addition to the 240 hours for removing and replacing the castings within the wing.

57

This is the work area in Building 10 at NASM's Preservation and Storage facility in which *Excalibur III* was restored. A number of specialists took part in this project, using their particular skills. This view, taken on April 6, 1977, shows that the landing gear had already been painted prior to installation.

RIGHT:

Portions of the wing structure that were heavily damaged by corrosion were cut out and replaced by similar pieces. Here, Dale Bucy replaces a rib nose cap after it was dated and marked as not being an original part.

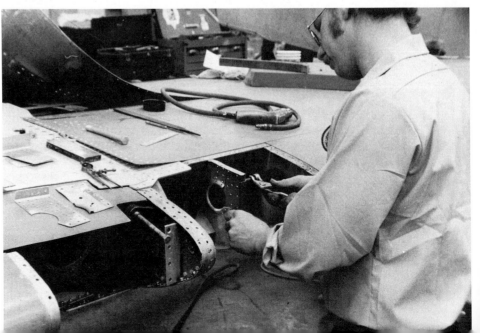

The manganese attachment castings for the landing gear were so badly corroded that they had to be removed and replaced. Curator for the Mustang's restoration, Robert Mikesh, points out to Charles Blair the damage caused by corrosion, during one of Blair's visits during the restoration. (Maureen O'Hara Blair)

The replacement castings needed repair because of previous hard usage. Attachment fittings that were broken off were salvaged from the original castings. Reid Ferguson, heading this P-51C restoration project, assists Harvey Napier, shop machinist, in making an alignment jig to hold parts during welding in January 1977.

One of the two repaired castings is shown in place within the wing, ready to be attached. The forward ears on the castings act as attachment pivots for the landing-gear strut fairings and were the portions that had to be fitted and welded in place.

Now that the wing structure was again opened during this casting removal, other areas of the internal structure were found to have corroded areas. Again, more skin panels had to be removed so that sections of ribs and structural members could be treated or cut out and replaced. The dust cover area at the rear of the wing in front of the aileron also had to be repaired because of hidden corrosion. In all, these internal structural repairs added another unprogrammed 250 man-hours.

A lesson learned in this operation was that as dedicated as general airframe companies may be in their specialized work, they should not be expected to be oriented, as is a museum, toward preservation of the technology on an airplane that will not be flown. Restoration practices encountered outside the professional museum field are limited primarily to enhancing the exterior appearance. The zinc chromate coating applied by the first contractor covered many traces of corrosion that would otherwise have been detected much earlier. When museum technicians finally closed the wing, they were satisfied that corrosion of internal parts was arrested, and that the integrity of the wing was complete to the last detail, including original-type rivets. The fuel

When the wing structure was completed, body filler was applied to build up low areas as Paul Mantz had done when originally modifying this P-51C as a racer. Karl Heinzel uses an air-powered sander to smooth the surfaces.

system of three separate fuel areas was retained, as it had been modified by the Paul Mantz Air Service, and a major objective of this wing restoration was thus met.

Restoration of the landing gear consisted of cleaning each part separately, and coating the inner walls of the struts with Soft Seal preservative. Metal spacers were placed inside the shock struts so that the air pressure could be released, yet the struts would remain at the correct extension.

In addition to the restoration work performed by outside contractors and the preliminary work accomplished in 1962, this final effort in wing restoration consumed 2,136 hours.

Renovating the Fuselage

Very little restoration work was required for the fuselage after the paint was removed and its metal structure and skin were chemically treated for corrosion prevention. This work was accomplished during the first period of restoration. Particular care was given to the removal of all loose and crusted dirt that often gathers on the inside of the aft and lower portion of the fuselage. This detail is often overlooked in nonprofessional restorations, and the presence of dirt encourages further corrosion, suggesting that a hasty and partial restoration without preservation was the objective.

During the resumed restoration, there were suspicions that the glycol radiator had not been previously removed for preservation. Consequently, the arduous task of disconnecting and lowering this heavy unit was under-

RIGHT:

The P-51's fuselage looks rather empty with the heavy components of the glycol cooler and oil cooler removed. Removing the wing and cooler components simplified cockpit restoration by allowing access through the bottom.

This air scoop venturi unit is fully restored and ready for installation. Viewed from the rear, the unit attaches to the front of the rectangular-shaped glycol-cooling radiator mounted under the fuselage. The oil cooler is in place at the bottom.

RIGHT:

This is a front view of the unit shown above. The oval radiator at bottom is the oil cooler. Air passing through this venturi goes into the glycol cooler at rear.

Components for the fuselage of this P-51C begin to go in place. Carroll Dorsey attaches the pipes and fittings needed for a complete and operating cooling system. Interior corrosion and rust were removed, and the interior tubing walls of all parts were covered with a preservative coating for long-term protection.

taken. This was a wise decision, for it was discovered, as suspected, that this phase had not been accomplished. The top and bottom caps were removed for easier cleaning and corrosion treatment of the caps and radiator core. They were cleaned with an alkaline cleaner, then dipped in copper brightener. Parts and core tubing were then coated with Soft Seal. Finally, the unit was sealed against outside moisture and reinstalled in the lower fuselage.

For unknown reasons, the 12.5-gallon oil tank that had been removed from the fuselage during the first phase of this restoration had disappeared during the fourteen years of inactivity. Also missing were the two 5-gallon auxiliary oil tanks that had been added to increase the aircraft's range. There is no record of what these smaller tanks looked like, and therefore they could not be duplicated for this restoration. P-51 oil tanks were basically standard, and one was purchased, along with the wheel castings, for this installation.

Other components, such as the tail wheel and control linkages, were removed, preserved, restored, and reinstalled. Effort was also directed to the engine mount and fire-wall area because of considerable corrosion there. Work on the fuselage and these components required 1,075.5 man-hours.

RIGHT:

The fuselage of the P-51C was given a number of coats of primer surfacer to fill in the skin seam lines, as Mantz had done in 1946. The surface sanding process raised considerable dust, and was accomplished outside the museum shop.

To arrest all corrosion and repair damaged portions, an expert sheet-metal specialist is essential for a complete restoration. One of the many repairs to the structure of Excalibur III is being made here by George Genotti, who also checked to ensure that all sheet-metal work was accomplished properly.

RIGHT:

The landing-gear wheel-well door is examined in its completed state by Charles Blair (center) and Robert Mikesh (right), curator for the restoration project. Reid Ferguson (left), one of the senior restoration technicians for the museum, headed the restoration of Excalibur III. (Maureen O'Hara Blair)

Cockpit photos of Excalibur III show comparison of before and after restoration. The airplane was received in a fairly complete condition, which eased the project considerably. The main effort in the cockpit was directed toward cleaning and repainting, not to factory freshness but rather to match its appearance when it was actively flying.

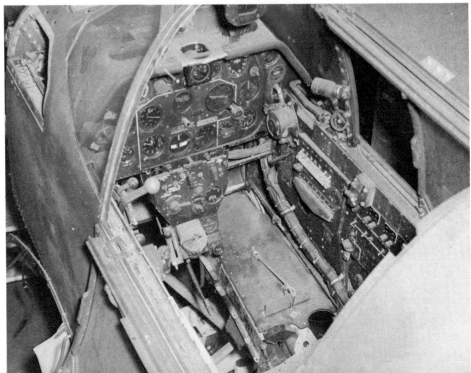

Detailing the Cockpit

The National Air and Space Museum devotes considerable attention to the exactness and detail of cockpit areas in aircraft restoration projects. Except for the engine and the aerodynamic design of an airplane, it is the completed cockpit with its equipment that reflects much of the technology of aviation for the time period of that craft.

The cockpit of *Excalibur III* has been restored as closely as possible to its configuration during the history-making polar flight. It is far more densely packed with avionics equipment than it was when this P-51C operated as an Army Air Force fighter. In addition to the standard equipment, the following avionics were added for the New York to London and the polar flights:

These photos serve as a comparison to show the original configuration in which P-51Cs left the factory when they were new in 1944. To the left is the standard instrument-panel arrangement and at right is a view of the right side of a factory-fresh P-51C. (Rockwell International)

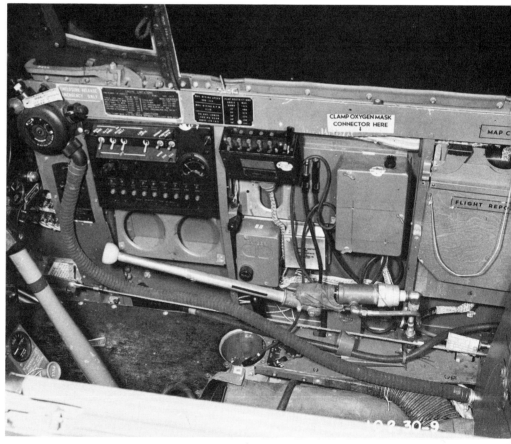

Two ADF-12B automatic direction finders

Two LR5-B VHF receivers

Two 12-channel RT10-C VHF transmitters

A special low-frequency transmitter with one crystal frequency at approximately 5,900 KC, with self-contained battery

Lear L-2C automatic pilot with YAW trim indicator

A special 3.5-to-6-megacycle medium frequency receiver, similar to LRA-5

Master direction indicator

Hand-reel and trailing antenna assembly

This assortment of electronics equipment was loaned and installed in *Excalibur III* for these flights by Lear, Inc., and returned to the company following the airplane's retirement. To ensure the completeness of the Mustang when it was donated to NASM, William Lear, president of Lear, Inc., donated the equipment to the museum so it could again become a part of this famous airplane.

Fighter aircraft cockpits are difficult to work in because of their small size. With the wing of *Excalibur III* removed, the bottom of the cockpit is left open. The special jig holding the fuselage was of such a height that technicians could stand upright and comfortably have access to most areas of the cockpit. The installation of equipment and cockpit restoration required 344 man-hours.

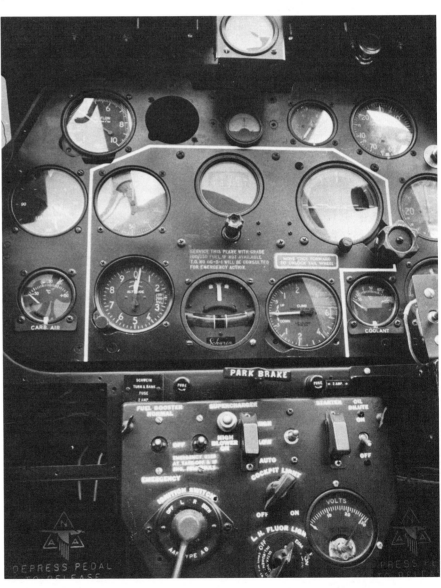

These photographs were taken soon after Captain Blair had flown his historic over-the-pole flight in Excalibur III. *An interesting comparison can be made of the instrument arrangement (above) as compared to the factory configuration on page 65. The photo below shows the unusual location of the two Lear VHF LR-5B radios, mounted inverted so that the pilot can tune them as he views them between his knees. There was no other place in the small cockpit for this relatively large equipment. One unit contains the tuning control of the Lear preselected twelve-channel RT10-C VHF radio. The two units mounted on their side in the center under the seat are control heads for the Lear "Orienter" ADF Model 12s. (C. F. Blair)*

This was the final configuration of the instrument panel for Excalibur III. Nonstandard instruments included the fuel-flow meter at upper left, which required relocating the compass to the overhead position of the windscreen. Also added was the Lear "Orienter" ADF dual reading instrument at left center. The six basic flight instruments are surrounded by a white border grouped in the center of the panel, a common marking practice in the forties and fifties.

The left side of the cockpit remained fairly standard. Brackets with wing nuts at the rear of the throttle handle (center) were repeated on the right side, and were used for holding the sextant support crossbar that was positioned in front of the pilot. This unit was easily removed and stowed. The bracket forward of the throttle was for holding the sextant when not in use. Landing-gear operating handle is at lower center; flap handle at left rear.

The right side of the cockpit shows a considerably cleaner arrangement than the military version. Much of this is accounted for by the elimination of unneeded military equipment. The hand-cranked reel at lower center was for a specially installed trailing antenna assembly.

The left side of the P-51 cockpit contains aircraft power controls and trim adjustment knobs. Attached at the side of this canopy rail is the sextant holding the bracket that Blair used for his polar flight.

The restored cockpit of Excalibur III was returned to the configuration it had for the polar flight. Lear autopilot controls are at the far right.

Most of the electrical controls of this P-51C are positioned on the right side of the cockpit. As a civil airplane, commercial equipment replaced unnecessary military electronics gear.

Fabric for the Empennage

Cleaning and restoration of these assemblies followed procedures already discussed, and had been accomplished during the first period of this project. Fabric surfaces were the only addition, and these were made of Grade A cotton. Stitches used for this fabric application were the same as those of the 1940s for military aircraft. This concluding work of applying the fabric on the empennage took 133 man-hours.

Despite the fact that the fabric on flight-control surfaces appeared to be in excellent condition, it was stripped off for structural cleaning. There were traces of metal corrosion that were then arrested, and the structure was repainted for future protection. This again justified museum policy that all fabric surfaces are to be removed on any aircraft being restored. This view of Excalibur III's *rudder shows it ready for a new fabric covering.*

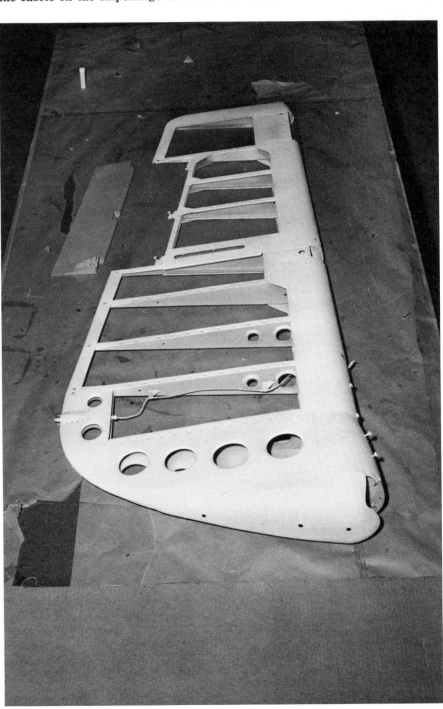

Admiring the workmanship of the restored Merlin, Charles Blair (right) recalled the reliability of this engine that allowed him to break, and continue to hold, the transatlantic speed record for aircraft of this class, and then to carry him safely nonstop across the North Pole from Norway to Alaska, and on to New York. (Maureen O'Hara Blair)

RIGHT:

The Rolls-Royce Merlin V-1650-9 engine of Excalibur III *was restored to like-new condition. The one exception was that preservatives were added to coat internal engine walls for prolonged protection. Most of the engine work was done by Patricia Williams, who specializes in the restoration of engines and propeller systems.*

Preserving the Engine

The complete breakdown of an engine of this type is seldom necessary if engine oil was retained while the airplane awaited restoration. For restoring this Rolls Royce Merlin engine, an internal inspection was made by means of a Boroscope placed through engine openings to search for possible damage, rust, and corrosion. The Merlin was in good condition, so standard preservation and restoration practices were followed. The engine was placed on a specially built mount that would allow it to be turned to any angle. Engine oil was drained, and the inner walls were then coated with a preservative. This material is sprayed through every engine opening so as to reach all internal walls and surfaces. The material used remains soft, yet will not run; consequently, if the engine should inadvertently be turned, the preservative will not be completely scraped away from cylinder walls. Engine openings were then sealed against moisture and the leaking of residual oil and excess preservative fluids. New exhaust pipe gaskets were made, leaving their centers unopened to serve as an exhaust port seal. Original-type spark plugs were used in lieu of Protek plugs for a tighter engine seal.

All accessories were removed, cleaned, and preserved, as necessary, then painted and installed. Exposed steel parts were cadmium plated, then sprayed with a clear coating for protection against rust. The exterior of the engine was also thoroughly cleaned and then repainted. Bright metal pieces such as tubing, nuts, and bolts received a little more attention in brightening to give that extra professional touch that Rolls-Royce people like to see.

It took 230 man-hours to make this engine ready for installation.

70

Finish and Assembly

On the surface, the painting of an aircraft would seem to be the easiest task of a restoration. The work itself is not all that difficult, but achieving accuracy in color and markings, when compared to the airplane's original state, can sometimes be very challenging. Any discrepancy is often noticeable and can negate much of the effectiveness of the total restoration effort.

A problem area encountered in the restoration of *Excalibur III* was in determining the original red color. At first it seemed a simple matter to use existing samples of the color to match new paint, but further consideration proved this to be invalid. The original paint that was applied in 1950 was an enamel with a linseed oil base, which darkens with time. The red sample taken from *Excalibur III* at the time of restoration was best described as a deep maroon, with a bluish cast and very little red luster. It was matched to Munsell 7.5R 2/6.

The final touches of red are put on the fuselage of Excalibur III *by Karl Heinzel in the museum shop spray booth. An acrylic lacquer was used, since it is easier to repair than enamel surfaces if scratches and chips should occur during moving and assembly for exhibit.*

The final coat of red acrylic lacquer receives a pneumatic wheel buffing from John Cusack before hand waxing. Both Mantz and Blair kept a high luster on this P-51C. The Lear autopilot and an oxygen tank can be seen through the open hatch on the side of the fuselage.

Museum technicians would prefer to construct the markings graphically and silk screen them on an airplane to achieve flawless reproduction. This is not done, however, with original work that is to be duplicated. Lawrence Motz takes on the difficult task of matching the original free-hand, brushed-on details of the American flag on the side of Excalibur III.

RIGHT:
Fitting the fuselage to the wing of Excalibur III was a tedious operation because of the many parts that had to mate. Reid Ferguson (left) aligns tubing, while Walter Roderick, shop foreman, directs the lowering of the fuselage.

Detail photo of the P-51C landing gear also shows the landing light, which was in the left wheel well only.

RIGHT:

Red and white diagonal stripes are distinctive marks for Excalibur III. *The rubber funnel-shaped object at the base of the rudder post is attached to the end of the trailing wire antenna.*

A laboratory analysis of the paint sample was in order, and help was requested of Randolph Products Company, manufacturers of aircraft finishes that dated back well before this time period. The thought was that, after the analysis, this company might have records of colors available in the 1950s to match their findings.

The color sample was placed in a spectrophotometer and wave curves were made on the original pigments used. From this information, the paint laboratory was able to compare the sample with materials that were in use at the earlier time period. The wave curves exactly matched those of Randolph Wine Red B-9164, also known as Stinson Red Q-1913. The only exception was in the darkness of the sample, and this was explained by the aging effect of the oil base.

This color was very common back in the later forties and early fifties, when it was used by many aircraft manufacturers, although it was not necessarily known by the same color names. This analysis was time-consuming, but with the evidence at hand it gave confidence that *Excalibur III* would again be in its original color.

A new paint with a Munsell equivalent of 7.5R 3/9 was acquired in acrylic lacquer. This deviation from the original enamel was justified by the fact that in moving, assembly, and disassembly of museum aircraft, there is frequent need of touching up, and lacquer is better for this type of maintenance.

The airplane was painted in disassembled form for several reasons. Aside from the fact that the assembled aircraft would not fit into the paint booth, tail surfaces and wing could be placed in more convenient positions for painting. It was also much easier to paint various marking details.

When the paint was completely dry, rubbing compound and wax were used to give a final smoothness and luster that this well-groomed, high-performance airplane must have had under its former owners.

Another victorious wave is given by Charlie Blair as he once again sits in this history-making cockpit at the conclusion of Excalibur III's restoration.

RIGHT:

Sharing interest with Charlie Blair in the restoration of Excalibur III was his wife, motion picture star Maureen O'Hara. This picture was taken at Foynes, Ireland, on July 8, 1976, on the occasion of the first flying-boat crossing of the North Atlantic since 1947; another first for Blair. The aircraft was Antilles Air Boats' Short S-25 Sandringham, Southern Cross.

Assembly was routine, and after a period of nearly nineteen years, during which the components had been disassembled, *Excalibur III* was once again a complete airplane. This phase of the Finish and Assembly required 361 man-hours. Many would-be restorers of aircraft consider only this final phase as consisting of a complete restoration. For *Excalibur III* this work amounted to 6 percent of the recorded man-hours expended in the museum shop. The one-year effort in completing the restoration consumed 4,288 man-hours, bringing the total to 5,679 hours, not including the work performed by outside contractors.

On October 19, 1977, the restoration of *Excalibur III* was officially completed. For all those who had a part in the effort, it was a joyous day when the glistening airplane was rolled out into the sunlight for the taking of photographs. In the open air, it looked every inch the great and historic airplane that it is. One member of the team was absent from the spirited gathering at the end of a long project. He was Charlie Blair, who was informed of the completion of *Excalibur III*'s restoration by phone at his home in the U.S. Virgin Islands. He expressed joyous relief; his "little red airplane" had come a long way!

The North American P-51C Excalibur III *is shown here in October 1977, after almost 6,000 hours of work restored it to near-new condition and assured its preservation.*

ABOUT THE AUTHOR:

Robert C. Mikesh is associate curator of aeronautics at the Smithsonian Institution's National Air and Space Museum. He served with the U.S. Air Force for twenty-one years, during which time he flew Douglas B-26 night intruders in Korea and Cessna O-2As as a Forward Air Controller in Vietnam. Most of his flying experience, however, was in Martin B-57 Canberra bombers. After retiring from the Air Force, Mr. Mikesh fulfilled a near lifetime ambition by joining the staff of the National Air and Space Museum. He is the author of *Japan's World War II Bombing Balloon Attacks on North America* in the Smithsonian Annals of Flight series, and is a frequent contributor to aviation periodicals, specializing in Japanese aviation history.